D0408366

BLOWING MY WAY TO THE TOP

How to Break
the Rules,
Find Your
Purpose, and
Create the Life
and Career
You Deserve

HARPER WAVE
An Imprint of HarperCollinsPublishers

BLOWING MY WAY TO THE TOP

JEN ATKIN

The photograph of the author with Gwen Stefani
on page 238 is courtesy of Sophie Muller.

All other images are courtesy of the author.

HarperCollins books may be purchased for educational, business, or sales promotional use. For information, please email the Special Markets Department at SPsales@harpercollins.com.

FIRST EDITION

Designed by Bonni Leon-Berman

Endpaper images courtesy of the author

Library of Congress Cataloging-in-Publication Data has been applied for.

ISBN 978-0-06-294055-1

20 21 22 23 24   LSC   10 9 8 7 6 5 4 3 2 1

For Dale and Chris Atkin, who, by adopting a little brown girl, gave me the opportunities that allowed me to follow my dreams. Thank you for your moral compass and your unconditional love. I'm sorry I cared more about my John Stamos posters than I ever did about Bible study.

Being featured in the *New York Times* changed my life forever—2015

CONTENTS

BLOWING MY WAY TO THE TOP

My first muse, Marci Atkin—1988

Backstage with Reshma Gajjar on Madonna's tour—2006

On the set of "Roar" with Katy Perry—2013

INTRODUCTION

When I first started out as a hairstylist, if I wanted to document my work I had to bring a camera with me to the job, snap pics, then go to Costco and get prints developed (doubles, of course, so I had an extra set to give to my client). Instagram didn't exist, and most stylists were reluctant to reveal their techniques or the lessons they'd learned on the road to success. The idea of giving hair tutorials to fellow stylists, let alone the public at large, was basically unheard-of. If anything, hairstyling was steeped in a culture of secrecy, because hoarding skills (and who you knew) was how you scored highly coveted jobs and kept the next generation from nipping at your heels. When I moved to L.A. in 2000, no one—or at least very few people—wanted to show me the ropes. It was hard, it was scary, and it was lonely.

I remember thinking back then that if my career took off, I wanted to do my small part to help change the professional culture. Instead of being competitive, I wanted to be collaborative. I felt a responsibility to share my story; I wanted to teach and pass along the knowledge I'd gained, whether it was how to work a curling iron and a pair of scissors or the lessons I'd learned the hard way about navigating L.A. when you're a nineteen-year-old ex-Mormon with no job and three hundred dollars to your name. When we share our trade skills, we all become better artists. When we share our life stories, we all become better people.

When Instagram finally did come around, about a decade after I arrived in California, I was an early adopter, showcasing cool hairstyles, inspo pics, and the technical tricks I'd picked up over the years. And as my followers grew—because people were sharing my photos with their friends and my clients were tagging me in their own pics—my work expanded by leaps and bounds and my life changed in ways I never could have anticipated. As I continued to build my hairstyling business and later launch my own products, I kept accumulating more knowledge that I wanted to share with people. About how to build a business and start a brand, how to forge meaningful relationships, how to embrace the art of the hustle, and how to question the people who don't want you to succeed. And most of all, how to go from feeling stuck in a life that isn't right for you to beating the odds and landing in a place where you can confidently say you feel like you've made it.

I've posted some of these life lessons on Instagram, Snapchat, YouTube, and my all-things-hair website, Mane Addicts. Now I'm collecting them in this book, because often the full stories are just too long for an Insta caption, and because I have a ton of respect for the life-changing magic of reading a book (I swear I own half the self-help section). But also because for me, sharing has been a lifeline. The few people who *were* kind enough to take me under their wing changed my life. If there's anything my experience with social media has taught me it's that being authentic and honest and opening up pays back in dividends. My career has been built on blood, sweat, tears, and hard work, but also on community. On human connection.

It took decades for me to muster the confidence to share the lessons I've learned in a book, or to even believe I had the authority to write a book, but I feel equipped today to help anyone who's in the place where I was twenty years ago: broke, scared, stuck, and wanting more out of life than what my community envisioned for me. I'll tell you the story of how I got from there to where I am today, a forty-year-old woman who's built a rewarding career, found financial security, and, even more importantly, has created the life she dreamed of. Of course, I'm not finished. I'm still learning and growing. But my life has changed so much that I do believe some of those early chapters have finally closed, and I can look back on them and share my discoveries—and bumps in the road—with candor, transparency, and hopefully a little bit of humor. (It wasn't always glamorous, believe me.) I'm excited to tell my story, and even more excited to help YOU discover *your* story and your best life ahead. Because you may not want to be a hairstylist, and building a product line might be the furthest thing from your mind, but we all want to live the life we were meant for. That's universal. We all want to have a life full of purpose. We want to feel loved and find success, however we define it.

THE QUESTION I GET asked more than any other is: *How did you get your start?** It's a good question, because I grew up very far from the life I lead now. I didn't know anyone when I arrived in L.A. I didn't have high-profile connections who could make career-changing introductions. I didn't even go to college. I grew up in Hawaii and Utah, the middle sister of three girls. I was the rule-breaking adopted daughter in a Mormon family where my life was planned for me at an early age. Both of my obedient sisters served Mormon missions† for two years. All I served was major attitude. I was supposed to graduate high school and seminary class, stay away from R-rated movies and explicit lyrics, and, upon turning eighteen, quit my job at Little Caesars and marry my high school boyfriend (after he completed his Mormon mission) with the goal of starting a family by twenty-one. I was supposed to follow the teachings of the Church of Jesus Christ of Latter-day Saints or risk being banned to hell and deprived of my family FOR ALL TIME AND ETERNITY. Super-chill. It was either/or. NBD, right?

By the time I was a teenager, I had developed what I like to call the Little Mermaid Syndrome. I wanted more. I wanted to be . . . *part of that world.* And by "that world" I mean the non-Mormon world, the one I saw on MTV and

---

* *Actually, I get three questions:* How did you get your start? How can I get to work with celebrities? *And:* Does your husband have a brother? *The answer to the latter two:* The same way you get to do anything—by working hard and being a good person. *And:* No, just a sister. And sorry, she's married.

† *Basically a service trip where you knock on doors (think* The Book of Mormon) *and volunteer doing humanitarian and church work.*

read about in *Tiger Beat* but couldn't be a part of myself. I was so curious about who I really was and what I was meant to be. And I was absolutely fascinated by stories of beauty and transformation. If a movie didn't have a makeover scene or a shopping montage, I wasn't interested. I loved music, fashion, and pop culture. While my friends were memorizing Scripture, I was buying *Bop* magazine to get the fold-out posters of New Kids on the Block and Paula Abdul.

Growing up, the only salons I knew of were located in suburban strip malls. But still I loved tagging along with my mom for her weekly appointments at Supercuts, Fantastic Sams, or, my personal favorite, United Hairlines. She would get a perm and then get her hair set, and she always had her nails done. I still remember the smell of the perm—I could have watched the stylists work on her hair for hours. No matter what my mother was doing, even if she had zero plans that day, she always got herself dressed nicely and put on a full face of makeup, and I saw how that changed her mood.* She'd wake up feeling blah, get glammed, and instantly have a better attitude. I definitely absorbed the idea that there was power in looking your best to feel your best, but it never occurred to me that it was even possible for me to be a hairstylist.

From what I saw all around me, not to mention in the movies (like *Edward Scissorhands* and *Shampoo*), hairstylists were white men. But I was definitely into doing my

---

* *During the COVID-19 pandemic, I would FaceTime my parents and my mom always had on her whole look, eyeliner included. She was literally all dressed up with nowhere to go.*

Barbies' hair, my little sister, Marci's, hair, and eventually my own. I was also obsessed with the hair books they used to have on display in salons. They were basically catalogues of different styles, with all these outrageous colors and shapes and angles. They were totally cheesy, but I could flip through them for hours. When I started out as a hairstylist, I had binders of "short," "medium," and "long" looks that I realize now were heavily influenced by these books.

I begged my mom for a perm like hers, to no avail, so I started putting my hair into a million tiny braids all over my head before bedtime. I'd sleep on them (not comfortable, in case you're wondering), and then brush them out in the morning for perfect waves. I was the fake-perm queen of my second-grade class. I loved playing with hairstyles, clothes, and makeup, and testing my creativity—but I didn't see any female role models in the salon world or even the larger business world in my community. Women were meant to be moms and wives and Relief Society members.* Being a professional hairstylist just wasn't on my vision board. Or it wouldn't have been, had I known what vision boards were back then. Hello Kitty didn't make them.

In the summer of 1999, after I graduated from high school, I moved with my best friend, Lindsay, from our hometown of St. George, Utah, to the big scary metropolis of Salt Lake City. Lindsay was basically the only person to ever understand me, and today we're twenty-eight BFF-years strong. I knew by then that I didn't want to be in Utah anymore, or attend church, but I was scared to leave

* *Google it.*

my family and my Mormon friends, and terrified of disappointing my parents and community back home.

At the time, my boyfriend was in Sacramento serving on his Mormon mission, and his mother was in Oklahoma working as a producer on a movie version of the classic children's novel book *Where the Red Fern Grows*. It starred . . . wait for it . . . Dave friggin' Matthews in his movie debut. Lindsay and I were HUGE Dave Matthews Band fans. (Who wasn't, in 1999? If you are not familiar with this Music for the Ages, I suggest starting with the album *Crash* and the hit song "Ants Marching.") We were invited to go visit the set, and we could not believe that we had the opportunity to be in such close proximity to a celebrity. We went to Oklahoma immediately, though I'm still confused as to how we paid the airfare, because neither of us had a credit card.

Guys, it was magical. It was transformative. We hung around the set and eventually got to take some embarrassing fangirl photos and have a few convos with Dave. We hung on every word he said. (To be clear, it was all very PG, you pervs.) He asked us about what we wanted to do with our lives, and who we wanted to be, and I remember being really honest with him, revealing out loud for the first time that what I wanted more than anything was to move to L.A. or New York. I told him that I wanted to work behind the scenes in movies or in a salon, and he just looked at me and said, "Then you should." Listen, I know it sounds a little ridiculous now, but I'm totally serious when I say it was that bit of encouragement from someone truly successful, someone I idolized, that changed the course of my life. Lindsay and I went back to our Motel 6 room that night totally giddy. Dave just gave us permission to take control of our destiny and told us to pursue our dreams?!?

Dave Matthews: 1. Joseph Smith: 0.

After that life-changing encounter, Lindsay and I got out of our lease in Salt Lake City and got in the car, probably blasting the Backstreet Boys' "I Want It That Way," and headed to California with zero plans, zero connections, and zero Wi-Fi, because it didn't exist. The one thing we knew was that we didn't want to get married and have kids yet. We wanted to live life outside our bubble and meet new people and experience the world.

Our parents? They were scared for sure—what they knew of Los Angeles was exactly what they didn't want for their daughters. The way they saw it, we were going to end up either as strippers or drug addicts, and our rejection of their lifestyle certainly tested their unconditional love—but for the most part, they stuck by us. They didn't exactly give us a going-away party, but they didn't disown us, either, which was a legitimate concern. Looking back now, I am so grateful to them for that unconditional love. It allowed me to start my new life with confidence and a clean slate, and it saved me a lot of heartache and money on therapy.

Our community, on the other hand, was considerably less supportive of our decision. The girls I'd gone to high school with were all marrying their high school boyfriends and moving into houses. Imagine an army of clones of Amanda Bynes's character in *Easy A*, Mormon edition. A former classmate once approached my mother at the grocery store to say she was praying for me because she'd heard I'd gotten into "self-worshipping." To my parents' credit, they may not have understood the life I'd chosen, but they stood by me and stood up for me. They took a lot of heat because of my choices.

Has it always been easy? Of course not. There have definitely been times when our relationship became a bit strained, but we've always found our way back, and we remain close. My mother has always loved me for who I am, even if what I've wanted for myself is different from what she wanted for her own life. And while my dad definitely had a specific plan for me, deep down he always wanted his girls to know that there was a bigger world out there beyond Utah. I am so grateful to both of them every single day.

Once Lindsay and I made the decision to leave, there was no turning back. Two decades later I think about my nineteen-year-old self—my platform Rocket Dog–wearing nineteen-year-old self—and I can see all the things that could have gone wrong, but at the time I just thought, *Let's do this.* I knew L.A. would offer more opportunities than Utah ever could, and that's all I wanted. A chance to have my own life. Keep in mind, at that point I'd never had a Black friend (and very few brown, tbh), I didn't know anyone who was L, G, B, T or Q,* and I barely knew what a Jewish or Persian person *was.* I didn't realize how lucky I had it, or what true struggles really looked like. But when you're bored of your small town you can start to feel sorry for yourself. Looking back now, I realize how privileged

* *Or, at least, none that were out to me. Maybe some of those male hairstylists I watched set my mom's hair were, but maybe not. It wasn't something I ever thought about, because I hardly even knew homosexuality existed.*

Lindsay and I both were, and how many things we didn't have to worry about that so many other people did. Just the fact that we were able to pick up and move to L.A. and feel like there was opportunity for us speaks volumes. We didn't know it then, but having loving parents, a safe upbringing, and the resources to do what we wanted was an incredible privilege. We didn't have the worry of taking care of our parents, and we weren't discriminated against based on our race or sexual orientation. Those struggles are real for many people in other communities, and I'll march and protest until my last breath to help bring social and racial justice to women and the LGBTQ and Black communities. But at eighteen I didn't have such a clear perspective, because I was young and because in 1998 none of us were as clearheaded about privilege and inequality as I hope we're becoming today (though there's still much work to be done).

As Lindsay and I drove out of Salt Lake City in our Honda Civic hatchback, we witnessed a crazy horrible accident—a semi had rolled over, hit a car, and burst into flames. I remember staring at the destruction, realizing that if we'd left ten seconds earlier that could have been us. Part of me worried that God was sending us a signal.

FOR A LONG TIME, my plan was to write a book once OUAI, the hair-care brand I founded, was, like, twenty years old. I wanted to have my Phil Knight *Shoe Dog* moment, but the reality is that that's not what my journey looks like. Mine's more of a "little brown Mormon girl shows up in L.A. and gets to work around amazing talent and in the best salons and backstage at New York Fashion Week and do the cover of *Vogue* with her idol Gwen Stefani and somehow launch a hair-care line" kind of story. Surviving and thriving for twenty years in this crazy town and crazy industry is my tale to tell.

When I look back on my career thus far, the thing that stands out is not what I've accomplished (and make no mistake, there have been failures in there as well) but the fact that I was not raised or educated for any of this. For the first twenty years of my life, I was not encouraged to forge my own path. I wasn't taught to be ambitious or venture outside of my homogenous Mormon community. Independence was discouraged, particularly for women. And I know I'm not the only one. You don't have to subscribe to a specific religion or be a certain age or part of a certain culture or live in a small town to feel like you want to bust out or change paths and create a new life for yourself. My hope is that this book will serve as inspiration for people who want to pursue a different life but don't think they can do it. If you don't have someone who offers you the support and the courage you need to go after the life you want, consider me your cheerleader.

My work in the salon is about helping to uplift people's self-image, but that goes beyond a blowout. When a client is in my chair, we aren't just talking about hair follicles or dandruff or how to use a flat iron. We're talking about who they think they are and what they want to do. For me, it took Dave Matthews saying "The world is your oyster, now go out and get it" (he could have written me a song, but beggars can't be choosers) to give me the boost I needed to go after my dreams. I want this book to do for you what Dave's words did for me. I hope that by the time you're done reading it, you have a renewed sense of who you are and who you deserve to be. I hope it helps you to conquer fear, drown out the expectations of society, release a self-image that's holding you back, and replace it with the self-confidence that allows you to find your voice. Because finding your voice is finding your power.*

Before we get started, a disclaimer: the people who know me best describe me as brutally honest and full of tough love. They're right, and that personality trait has served me well over the years. I believe in having the guts to speak up, question authority, and tell the truth rather than say what people want to hear. So now you know what's coming. It's real talk about success and how I got it. It will always come from a place of encouragement and positivity, and I hope it's what you want and need to hear, but I promise not to sugarcoat. No one has time for B.S.

So sit tight and let's get started.

---

* *Also, I hope Dave Matthews doesn't take out a restraining order on me.*

Hawaii—probably just a random dress-up Tuesday—1988

My second-grade May Day look in Oahu—1988

CHAPTER ONE
FEELING GOOD
AS HELL

I have been blessed in this life with a healthy dose of confidence. Not cockiness, mind you—the two are different—but a deep sense of my own value. Even when I was a new L.A. transplant crashing on other people's couches and parking two blocks away from the salon where I worked as a receptionist so no one would see my beat-up car, I never questioned myself or my abilities. I knew I'd have to bust my ass and that nothing would come easy, but I also knew I could get where I wanted to go (eventually). And just as importantly, I never felt *less than* anyone else. As I sat behind the desk welcoming the likes of Jessica Alba and staring at a revolving door of the rich and famous and drop-dead gorgeous, I didn't feel a sense of unworthiness; I felt inspired. This self-confidence has been a real asset over the years, and I always tell people that confidence is a necessary quality if you want to be successful. Because when things are especially hard or you feel especially beaten down, the only way to push yourself through is by believing you are as worthy of success as anyone else.*

I always joke that I was smother-loved as a child, that my parents never put me down, and that's why I'm so confident today. I was adopted at birth. My parents adopted me from an Ecuadorian girl who wanted to come to America to give her daughter a chance at a better life. She had to hide her pregnancy from her entire family, and I am forever grateful to her for that sacrifice and choice. My mom and dad always made every effort to ensure I knew that the very things that made me different—the fact that I didn't look like my sisters or my cousins, or that I was one of the only brown kids in our Utah town—were actually the things that made me special. And, to their credit, that message came through loud and clear. My poor husband definitely suffers because of their efforts.

Confidence was modeled to me by the women in my life for as long as I can remember. That might seem surprising, given that I grew up in a household where I was expected to get married and raise kids after high school and generally roll back my ambitions. But even in a community where the women were largely subservient to the men, confidence played a role for both genders. My grandma Atkin was as strong and tough as it gets, and very opinionated for a Mormon woman of her age. My favorite story of hers is about when my grandfather proposed. "Give me a week to think about it," she said. "I'll get back to you."

---

* *This isn't just my opinion—studies show that believing in yourself is as important as intelligence when it comes to finding success! Those same studies show that most women are woefully lacking when it comes to confidence. Just saying.*

I like to think I take after her.

My parents always taught me that I had the right to speak up for myself, and that I was smart and thoughtful and had ideas worth sharing. I know that may not sound especially progressive in today's culture, but you have to remember that we're talking about Utah in the 1980s. The values my parents instilled in me were a lot more progressive than what some of my classmates were hearing in their homes, and I don't underestimate the impact it's had on my life.

By the time I decided to leave Utah, I had enough confidence to know I had something to offer the world, but I didn't actually know what that was, which I found pretty frustrating. I knew, as I told Mr. Dave Matthews, that I wanted to work in movies or a salon, but I wasn't sure what exactly I'd do in either of those places. I had worked in the family travel agency, at a spa, at Little Caesars and—surprise, surprise—I had no passion. I had no specific goals, either. I didn't have a clear idea of what "success" looked like, and I didn't have a vision of being wealthy or influential. I was just determined not to live a life of disappointment. I didn't know what I wanted to do, but I knew I wanted to find happiness.*

Maybe you can relate—you know you want more from life, but you don't know what your future looks like or what your "thing" is. And that's perfectly okay. Maybe you're still figuring some shit out. You don't have to have all the

---

* *While writing this book, I've found so many photos of me doing my sisters' hair, my own hair, and even cutting friends' hair, but somehow I never realized back then that it was my true calling.*

answers. But you *do* have to know that you deserve happiness. You are worth the effort it will take to discover your calling.

BE SOMEONE WORTH BELIEVING IN

There's no getting around the fact that if you want to succeed at, well, anything, you need to embrace the art of self-promotion—and I'm not just talking about taking well-lit selfies and tagging your Instagram posts. People have been selling themselves forever—it's what resumes and job interviews are for. And dating apps, for that matter. And, before that, the classifieds.

My first real foray into self-promotion came when I was trying to get established as a hairstylist on the red-carpet circuit. I would fly myself to New York or France or wherever the big event was going to be (even though I could barely cover the airfare) and send emails to all my contacts—*Hi, I'm going to be at New York Fashion Week! Bonjour, I'm going to be in Cannes!*—and hope the work would come. Then, when Instagram took off, I immediately recognized its potential as a marketing tool. My industry is visually oriented, and here was the perfect medium for sharing images of my work with millions of people. I also think I had an advantage when it came to reaching new audiences; as a girl who grew up outside the Hollywood bubble, I understood how to connect with users from all over. I think I instinctively knew what people wanted to see, what they wanted more or less of—because I *was* them. Over time, I built a global audience on Instagram and gradually promoted myself. In 2014, when I launched Mane Addicts, my website for hairstylists and the hair-obsessed, the audience was already there and opted in.

A few years later, when I was trying to raise a second round of funding for my new hair-product line, OUAI (the first round came from a single investor; more on that in Chapter Five), I needed to put my promotional skills to use in a different way. Talent and followers and engagement alone weren't going to cut it. Building a business is a crazy beast. It takes real money, and I had to have a growth plan. I had to have the confidence to sit in front of venture capitalists and private equity groups and say, *Here's what I've built, here's what I want to do. It's going to be huge, and this is why you should give me your hard-earned cash . . . and lots of it.* I didn't go to college and I don't have a business background, and back then I didn't know the lingo, but I had to convince these VC guys—most of whom probably went to Stanford and Harvard and would rather give their money to dudes they graduated with than to a high school–educated hairstylist—that I was a good bet.*

I can still feel the nervous energy trickle down my spine when I think about showing up at those lunches and dinners and sitting down at a table full of men to pitch

---

* *I don't say "dudes" generically—less than 10 percent of the decision makers at venture capital firms are women, and only about 2 percent of VC dollars go to companies led by female founders (even less to companies with female founders of color). I still remember feeling disappointed that there weren't women calling me up to take a meeting. Trailblazers like Kirsten Green and Melinda Gates are working hard to change that, but for now it sure feels like Silicon Valley is a boys' club. Ladies, we've got ceilings to shatter.*

a hair-care line. (These meetings always take place over a meal so that asking for millions of dollars feels less intimidating. It's like a first date: you show up all cute, and it's almost immediately obvious if the chemistry isn't there and you're about to get rejected over text or voicemail in a few days.) And listen, I'm a realist. I know I had an easier time getting a foot in the door because I had "Kardashian-Jenner Stylist" in my title and I'd come up in Beverly Hills salons, but I absolutely felt the weight of all those eyes on me. Knowing that my connections helped me get the meeting only made me more determined to kill it, because I wanted to earn the investment. I wanted to make my clients and girlfriends proud and I didn't want to make any of the people who had helped me get those lunches look bad. I also felt an added pressure to show future female hairstylists that this was possible.

So I summoned my courage and confidence and reminded myself that I was an expert in my field—I had knowledge these guys didn't, and I understood and had access to a market that was hungry, loyal, and untapped. I had an authentic relationship with my followers that no other hair-care brand could claim, at least not in 2014. I took a seat at the table, in my favorite jeans, t-shirt, and blazer look (and obviously a good shoe), and presented my plans for further engaging the consumer and scaling the business and partnering with retailers like Sephora and Ulta, which would make it easier to eventually expand into other product categories. I looked them in the eye, answered their questions, and promoted my work, and I could tell by the men's rapt attention that I was hitting it out of the park. I felt like I was in the final scene of *Romy and Michele's High School Reunion.*[*]

It would have been very easy to walk into those meetings full of fear and self-doubt, nervously recite my presentation, and slink away. And if I had, I probably would have been underestimated. But I knew that if I wanted to grow the business I had such a clear vision for, I was going to have to sell myself as much as I sold my idea. Investors often say they invest in people, not companies, and I wanted to prove that I was someone worth believing in. So I talked up my years of experience on salon floors and working with celebrities and influencers and on editorial shoots and runways, because I wanted to prove that I know what works when it comes to hair products. I touted my growing social following, which allowed me to talk directly to consumers and learn what they were looking for from hair care. I schooled them on Mane Addicts and Mane University, where I invited top hairstylists to present to rooms full of eager newbies or seasoned professionals looking to refresh their technique, to show that I knew how to create and grow a brand and connect with my professional hairstylist audience as well as consumers.

I knew my worth.

I once heard Chelsea Handler say that women need to promote themselves the way they would their big sister or their friends, and that piece of advice has always stuck

---

[*] *Pro Tip: Studies show that eye contact communicates strength and self-control. Stare deep into someone's eyes if you're trying to make a connection or a sale.*

with me. Being confident doesn't make you self-centered. So many talented women I've met have trouble owning their success or abilities. They're embarrassed or they feel guilty or they don't want to be the center of attention, which makes sense since women have been taught for generations to put other people's needs ahead of our own. But you can champion yourself without abandoning the people around you, whether you're selling a product or yourself or an idea. On social media especially, we all have an audience, and in order for people to push that Follow button, they need to think you're special, so you need to believe that, too.

That said, I feel like I need to issue the following PSA: please remember that there is a *big* difference between championing yourself and being cocky. Cockiness is arrogance. It's believing—or at least, posturing—that you are somehow better/smarter/more successful/cooler/hotter than other people. Unfortunately, the competitive, look-at-me culture of social media can make it a little too easy for that line to get blurry. Before you hit Post on anything, do a gut check. Are you showing up or showing off? Not only is arrogance an ugly trait, it's a self-defeating one: when you think you know everything, you cheat yourself out of opportunities to improve. And becoming a know-it-all is a really quick way to make mentors and other valuable connections want nothing to do with you. Just think about it—do *you* want to invest your valuable time in someone who thinks they've already got it all figured out?

Confidence is the opposite of cockiness. When I was twenty-eight and starting to move beyond what people thought of as "assisting age," I made the choice to stick with it and keep eating ramen because I wanted to learn about editorial and runway hairstyling from the best peo-ple I could. *That* took confidence. Finding yourself in an unfamiliar position and saying "I actually don't know how to do this—can you show me?" is confidence. Cockiness is putting on airs to cover up your insecurities, trying to prove you know everything in an attempt to mask your fears or uncertainties. Cockiness is rushing through all the opportunities to learn in order to get to the next rung on the ladder, or saying "I got this" and then failing be-cause you were too arrogant to ask for help. This can hap-pen even to the most well-intentioned of us. Just last year I refused to use a teleprompter for a presentation because I thought I didn't need it . . . and then I missed an entire paragraph because I blanked in the moment. Oops. We all make mistakes, or get a little cocky sometimes—but when it happens over and over, when you don't learn from your mistakes but instead blame them on other people, then you need to check yourself (before you wreck your career).*

RISKY BUSINESS

Ask anyone you admire the story of their success and I can almost guarantee you that the most pivotal mo-ments will center around taking a risk. Sometimes those risks have a big payoff, and other times the immediate re-sult looks more like an epic failure, but no matter the short-term fallout, this is when the big change happens. I try to

---

* *Also, if someone is trying to give you advice, please do not interrupt them. It's one of my pet peeves.*

always remember that failure is the thing that has transformed some of the most successful people in history. You just need to focus on finding the opportunity for growth within the failure.

The riskiest decision I've ever made—to leave my hometown, my family, and the life that was planned for me in order to pursue an alternate path of my own making—is without a doubt the most rewarding choice I've ever made. Certainly it was a leap of faith, and I am very fortunate that it worked out the way it did, but the point is that there is no reward without risk. When you find yourself at a fork in the road, you have to be brave enough to take the uncertain path. It's your life, and deep down you know what you want from it. I encourage you to be honest with yourself: Are you following a path because you want to or because you're expected to? Are you playing it safe because you're happy or because you're afraid of failing, afraid of what other people might think?

I guess I'm lucky in this regard, because other people's opinions have never really kept me from doing the things I wanted to do. Sometimes I actually wonder if I'm missing the gene that would make me care what other people think of me. This ability to drown out the haters (and those can be family members, friends, or strangers on DM) has undoubtedly helped me follow my heart when it would have been easier to fall back on safer options. And with a little practice, it's a learnable skill.

If you consider yourself risk-averse, I encourage you to think of these pivotal moments less as scary leaps into the unknown and more as badass challenges. And start small—maybe don't jump in by moving across state lines with only a few hundred dollars and nowhere to live. If you're looking to switch careers, your first challenge might be to reach out to someone who works in your ideal field to ask some questions. If you want to start a business, gather the courage to share your idea with one person you trust. Next, start observing what other companies in the same space are up to. Eventually, you may want to develop a proof of concept and do some research to see if there's a market for what you're trying to sell. Once you get into the habit of pushing aside doubt and fear, you'll realize you have nothing to lose. There may be some misses along the way, but I really do believe in the saying that "rejection is God's protection."

I've been rejected more times than I can count. When I first tried to get a job in the hair industry, it took twenty salons saying NO before one said yes. There was the year I spent trying to get signed by an agent before most people even gave me the time of day. There were the lucrative spokesperson offers for hair companies that went to men time and time again. There were the publicists who didn't want me working with their clients because I wasn't cool enough or a big enough name. There were the many people who said no when I tried to sell them on the idea of my own product line. There was the ethnic blow-dry bar I invested in that never took off (more on that later, promise). There were the OUAI products we were totally psyched about that nose-dived at launch. Sometimes you can do your very best and listen to your inner voice and be true to yourself and make the bold move and . . . the timing won't be right and things won't work out the way you planned. But that's the biggest test of all. That's the moment you need to trust yourself and your vision and have the confidence to dust yourself off and figure it out and keep going. The alternative is feeling hopeless, giving up, or getting stuck.

I'd much rather take big risks and try new things and sometimes fail than take no risks at all. I don't want my career, or my business, to be about playing it safe. I know it's kind of a woo-woo idea but it's true that a lot of times when one door closes, another opens. When one thing doesn't work out, you can see more clearly where you should invest your talent and energy and, *voilà*, that's exactly where you were supposed to be all along. Try to remember that this experience is wild for everyone. There are hundreds of thousands of people in the world right now who are feeling the exact same way you are. It will get better (for all of us), so keep at it.

When people ask me how I got to where I am today, I think they're hoping that if they follow the same path, they'll reach the same result. Making a big change seems less risky if someone else has charted the course and made it through alive. But there's no blueprint for any of this; what seems like a risk to one person might seem like a luxury to another. When I look back on my journey, it feels to me like it was built on one risk after another. Taking the job to work backstage on Madonna's Confessions tour (yes, that happened) was a major leap, because I didn't have experience working with wigs or doing hair that had to stay put through hours of super-intense choreography. And if I had done a crappy job (can you imagine—a wig soaring across the stage in the middle of "Ray of Light"?), it could have been the end of my budding career.

A couple of years later, leaving the comfort of the salon floor—where I had established myself and developed a reliable business and was making a pretty good living—in order to work with John Galliano at Paris Fashion Week felt like a huge risk, because I hadn't been a part of that backstage fashion world and I felt like the odd American (wo)man out. Then I launched a digital hair platform and created a product line— what did I know about any of that? I had a vision, sure, but there was a pretty big leap involved.

I know these gigs probably sound fun and glamorous—and let's be real, they were—but they were also super-high-pressure and a ton of hard work. Messing up would have meant career disaster at a time when I could easily have been content as a hairstylist at a prestigious salon, with clients who kept coming back. It would have been a nice, safe living, and it was one that I could only have dreamed of back when I was a teenager in Utah. But I wanted to keep learning and growing, and I wanted to build myself as a person and as a brand. I wanted more for myself, and in the end that's what those critical risk-taking moments boil down to: wanting more for yourself, and wanting it so badly that you can't *not* go for it. The safe option starts to feel unsustainable, and life is just too short for that.[*]

It's important to note here that there's a big difference between taking a calculated risk and making a rash decision. Taking a risk does not mean up and quitting your job with no plan in place, and I would never suggest someone

---

[*] *On the flip side, ask me to jump into a cold pool and it takes me about thirty minutes to finally get there.*

do that. (I know, I know, I'm not the best example. But that's the thing about being nineteen—you're too young to be scared or responsible, and sometimes that works to your benefit. Sometimes.) The ability to take smart risks is honed over time. Call it trusting your gut, or listening to your inner voice. The Mormon Church calls it the Holy Ghost, Disney calls it Jiminy Cricket, I call it your true spiritual self. Whatever your name for that guiding force telling you to take the leap, it gets developed through the years, with each good or bad decision you make. You learn what works and what doesn't as you go, but that voice is always there, and if you can drown out the noise around you and really turn your gaze inward, it will pretty reliably guide you. Believe in yourself, believe that only *you* truly know what your life should be, and know that you are deserving and worthy of the life you want. There is something pretty incredible about looking back at both the wins and the failures without regret. I can tell you first-hand, it feels really, really good.

LET'S SET SOME BOUNDARIES

Sometimes I think there's no greater sign of confidence than saying no to a request—from a client, a friend, a family member, whomever. Saying no to someone else means that you know yourself, and you know your limits, and you know that just because you're saying no today doesn't mean you can't say yes tomorrow. Welcome to Boundaries.

I haven't always been good at saying no. When you work for yourself, or you're in more of a freelance line of work that relies on getting booked for jobs or winning contracts, there's a real fear that if you say no to an opportunity, the offers will stop coming. And that *is* a risk, and sometimes saying no means disappointing someone. But to succeed at anything, you have to know how to prioritize and how to invest your time and energy in ways that help you meet your goals—even if that means you have to let a few people down along the way.

I still have the spreadsheet I kept when I was just starting out on my own as a hairstylist. (It's been saved on my computer for fifteen years. Obsessive much?) I used it to document every single job I took on, and how much I made for each, year after year. When I look back at it now, I'm in awe of how hard I worked. But I'm also struck by the reality that I didn't *need* to work that hard. I didn't have to say yes to all of it. I could have given myself a break every now and then or focused on another part of my business, had a personal life, and still ended up where I am today. More often than not, you won't be penalized for saying no every once in a while—especially if you do so respectfully. People will understand, and if they don't, well, move on. It's far worse to say yes and then let someone down because you're overcommitted or overworked.

Setting boundaries takes practice. The more you do it, the more comfortable you will become, and you'll get better at saying no gracefully. These days, if I see a client who requested me for a job I couldn't do, I acknowledge it. "I'm so sorry I couldn't do your hair for that party/press junket/

premiere," I'll say. "But I hope it was a great event and that you were happy with your look!" I'm not defensive about the fact that I said no (protesting too much never helped anyone), and I'm not overly apologetic, either. People show you the respect you command. Setting clear boundaries gives you the space to focus on the things that will help you grow—whether that's saying no so you can get some much-needed rest or blocking off your calendar to catch up on paperwork and finances or to spend time with family. Be deliberate about how you invest your time.

In work environments, saying no often means passing up a paycheck—I don't want to pretend otherwise. But the long-term payoff can be worth the immediate sacrifice. In my career, there have been many opportunities that, had I taken them, would have made me too busy or over-committed to conquer the bigger projects that required my full attention. I feel very lucky to have gotten to a point where I can consider if any particular deal or job or partnership is right for me. If I was focused entirely on making everyone happy, I would have run myself ragged long ago.*

The same rules apply to the rest of your life, too. There will always be people who ask a lot of you, or who come to rely so much on your generosity or availability that it veers into the category of taking advantage—whether it's a sibling who keeps you on the phone for hours (and hours!) with their latest relationship drama, or colleagues who give you shit when you pass on happy hour in favor

---

* *Oh wait, I actually did run myself ragged a few years ago. More on that later.*

of a quiet night of self-care, or even the friends who don't understand when you have to decline a wedding invitation to avoid maxing out your credit card. Setting boundaries and saying no to people you care about can be scary, but it's also empowering. Everyone's limits are different, but knowing yours and respecting them takes confidence and strength. It also helps to manage other people's expectations. If you're constantly saying yes and taking on everything that's asked of you, there's no reason for anyone to expect any different. Take it from the woman who basically ran a one-person hair factory for six years straight. It's not sustainable.

These days, I'm getting more comfortable with saying no. I'm never an asshole about it, but creating boundaries around my availability shows people that I value myself and my time and my work. I hope they value those things, too. The next time someone asks you to do something that fills you with dread or resentment or makes you feel exhausted just thinking about it (and not the good *I-just-kicked-ass* kind of exhausted but the *I-have-no-more-left-to-give* exhausted), I urge you to politely say no. It will serve as a reminder to yourself that your needs matter. And most of the time, it ends up not being such a big deal for the other person. Or so my agent has told me.

HATERS GONNA HATE

What's the smartest business decision you've ever made?" That's another question I get asked pretty often, and the answer, for me, is obvious . . . and it has to do with saying yes to one of the most unexpectedly influential women of our time.

When I was offered the opportunity to work with the Kardashians, my agent discouraged it. *Why would you want to work with reality stars?* she asked. In her defense, this was 2011, and reality was *The Hills* and *Newlyweds.** *You should be working with high-profile actors and actresses. No one cares about reality-show people!* she said. Back then, reality stars weren't the royalty they are today and Hollywood was an even more elitist club.

But I didn't care whether or not they were considered A-list. The Kardashians were kind and smart and funny, and I enjoyed their company (plus they had amazing hair!), so I ignored my agent's advice. Also, I really vibed with Khloé, and she wrote me the sweetest email I've ever received, asking me to help her with her look for her first TV hosting gig. I recognized her good heart and incredible spirit early on. We all know how this story turns out. No one could have imagined what this family would become. And alongside their enormous success, they believed in lifting up the people around them. Kim was one of the first celebrities to recognize and tag her glam squad on Instagram. She wasn't just insanely gorgeous and fun and smart, with an amazing head of hair . . . she was all of that and *also* generous with her praise, and I credit the generosity of Kim, Kris, Khloé, Kourtney, Kylie, and Kendall for my career.

Suffice to say, saying yes to that single opportunity has

---

* *Also* The Simple Life, *one of the most brilliant TV shows in history.*

driven home for me how important it is to trust my gut and tune out opinions that just don't sit right. In this case, I know my agent had my best interests at heart—she was coming from a good place. At that time there was a blue-print for becoming a successful hairstylist, and it didn't involve working with reality TV stars. Unfortunately, some-times the opinions that get thrown at you come from con-siderably less respectable sources. Yes, I'm talking about haters.

You know what I'm going to say here: ignore the haters! But the reality is, ignoring negative, nasty voices is at times a lot easier said than done. As I grew my social following over the years, there were more eyes on me and, ugh, more people or accounts looking to tear me down. Usually this doesn't bother me too much and I don't engage, but in 2018, I found myself clapping back at someone for the first time. A controversial beauty reviewer wrote a mean post on Insta-gram about Kim Kardashian's KKW Body fragrance, not just critiquing the product but really attacking Kim's char-acter along with it. It isn't like me to respond to review-ers, but I jumped to my friend's defense, calling out what I saw as the hypocrisy of slamming Kim's contribution to consumerism while this person was making a living off reviewing those products. In hindsight, I probably should have stayed quiet. My comments got picked up by a few magazines and got called out by other bloggers, who said I was the one being cruel. It was the first time in my career that I've had to withstand that kind of public scrutiny of *me* as a person. It was pretty uncomfortable, tbh.

I tend to speak my mind when I feel like something

is unjust or someone is being picked on, and usually I'm proud of that quality. In this case, though, I realized it might have been a mistake. What I did just brought more attention to the negativity when I could have left it alone. Had I not learned from watching publicists handle this stuff for so many years? Still, there was no way to take back my comments, so I looked at it as a test of my confidence. It's easy to feel great about yourself when things are going well, but when your character is being questioned online and in the press, that's when you need to walk the walk. Ultimately, I knew I couldn't let what strangers were saying about me affect how I felt about myself, so I moved forward. And the good news, as my friend Virgil Abloh likes to say, is that "the world moves as fast as we scroll Instagram." The moment passed, and the beauty world moved on to the next story. Still, it was a good lesson for me in staying above the fray.

It's easy to get caught up in what people think or say or write about you online, or to get defensive and want to protect yourself or your friends by lashing out at trolls. On the road to success, if there's one thing I can promise you, it's that there will be many people who don't understand or agree with decisions you make. There will be people who unfollow you because they get sick of your posts or find your stories annoying or don't agree with your political views. I mean, we've all felt that way about an account at some point, whether it's personal or professional. (Thank you, Jesus, for that Mute button.)

In 2012, when I first started my Instagram account, my peers thought that I was being ridiculous. They would openly mock the fact that I was posting collages or behind-the-scenes videos, because I was usually the only one doing it. I had to have confidence to believe that I knew what I was doing and that I was onto something. I was able to drown out the haters because I always knew that if someone was bad-mouthing me, it wasn't actually about me. Usually that kind of criticism stems from people's own insecurity, so I tried to give them the benefit of the doubt and not let their frustration with themselves transfer to me. That old playground song—"I'm rubber, you're glue . . ."—was kind of spot on.

EVERYONE'S A CRITIC

Haters and trolls are not to be engaged with. But that doesn't mean you should walk around like a know-it-all with your fingers in your ears screaming "LALALA." Living in a bubble is a strategy that worked for no one, ever. Constructive criticism is essential for growth.

I run a hair-care brand. I create a product that is meant to serve people on a practical level, which means consumer feedback is super-important. In business, constructive criticism is valuable, and you have to be able to take that feedback as intended—not as disparagement but as a nudge to do better.

I'm always asking our customers what products they want to see and, more importantly, what existing products we could improve upon. For a while, a lot of people said that they wanted us to use more eco-friendly packaging, but we couldn't afford to source the materials. I hated that we couldn't do better, but the hard reality of business is that you can't always do what you want when you want. Still, I kept that idea in my back pocket, and as soon as we could afford to do so, we made a change—and we continue to make changes. As a brand founder, I care so much about what people have to say about our products. There's a big difference between changing who you are because you succumb to personal criticism, and adjusting your business or your goals in response to reasonable feedback.

During the racial injustice movement in June 2020, we got many questions about the diversity in our product range and messaging. George Floyd's murder sparked hard but important conversations, and as a company we took a look at how many Black employees we had on staff and discussed what we could do to increase diverse representation. The feedback from our community helped us bring positive change from within. We recognized our own shortcomings—and the shortcomings of the beauty industry as a whole—and took steps to prioritize diversity and inclusion into the culture at OUAI.

When it comes to OUAI, I'm trying to address a problem, and I need honest input to make that happen. I've never wanted to have a brand that was just about quick returns and fake relationships with consumers. My favorite question to ask my friends when they compliment a marketing asset or product is, "Yeah, but what *don't* you like about it?" You really commit to your own growth when you take the good and take the bad.

Like most of the lessons I've learned while building my company, this one extends far beyond business. Feedback is valuable in all its forms, and it requires a certain amount of confidence to take it in without becoming de-fensive. Maybe it's a comment from a friend about the per-son you're dating, or from a romantic partner who's noticed that you seem a little more down than usual. When my husband points out that I'm *still* working late into the eve-ning when I promised I'd spend quality time with him, or when friends mention that they haven't seen me in ages, I take that not as criticism that I suck at being a wife or friend but as honest feedback that I need to look at my schedule and reprioritize. I try not to get defensive and to really listen to them.

Feedback can help us understand what energy or im-pression we're putting out into the world. Sometimes you may get feedback, note it, and decide to dismiss it. And that's perfectly okay. You know yourself best. But having enough self-awareness and self-respect to at least take in someone else's perspective is critical if you're going to grow personally and professionally. If everybody had every-thing figured out all the time, no one would progress. And when someone you trust says something you *really* don't want to hear? Listen even harder. Do not shut them out or shut them down for having the courage to share something tough with you. It's easy to dismiss people and wall your-self off out of fear, but the reality is that trying to succeed solo is a recipe for disaster. Isolation is not good for human beings or businesses. We all need connection and a com-munity of people who care enough to be honest with us, even if we don't always like what they have to say. I mean, what's the alternative? Thinking "Why me?" while you binge-watch Netflix and catastrophize the world leads you nowhere, I'm sorry.

CONFIDENT WHILE FEMALE

While I truly believe that confidence should come from within, I'm also a hairstylist, so I know the power of a fresh cut to bring out the best in anyone. Looking good isn't everything, but feeling confident about the whole package—hair, outfit, makeup, all of it—is helpful, especially when you're trying to leave an impression.* Get out of the way of a woman who has stepped her shit all the way up.

I also know that finding inspiration in the confidence of others can help you channel a little bit of that energy for yourself. For me, those role models are usually badass trailblazing women. Whether I'm taking a cue from Kris Jenner's determination or Melinda Gates's service or Angela Davis's strength or Jane Fonda's activism, reminding myself of someone else's journey is often what I need to feel like I, too, can conquer the world. I really hope this book will do that for some of you. Maybe listen to Gwen Stefani or Beyoncé while you're reading it.

And remember: confidence changes over time. When I started out, nothing gave me a boost like getting the call for that next job. I just wanted to have steady work, get paid, and maybe one day "make it." Every offer I got felt like another sign that I was on my way. Today, while I'm still incredibly proud to be a working stylist, I'm even more excited about my ability to build and train a team. I revel in the pride I get from knowing I can trust someone from my team to do the jobs I can't, because that means I've had

---

* *If all else fails, a snatched bun and a red lip never fail.*

a positive influence. Being in demand means I have talent, but watching others in my orbit succeed means I have a legacy.

And yet the thing I often feel most compelled to apologize for is my own success. Not because I feel guilty for making it, but because I know I got there more quickly than others. Never for one second do I forget the hard work that other stylists before me put in and the barriers they've spent time breaking down. Nor do I forget the stylists who may have worked harder than others, but still were not granted certain opportunities or the same kind of success.

My career has moved quickly, largely because of technology, but also because of my own (and my clients') hustle. Still, sometimes I find myself wanting to shrug off the credit. Whenever I find myself making excuses for my success rather than taking responsibility for it, I have to give myself the same pep talk I'm giving you.

Own your success. You've earned it. Take confidence in it. And don't apologize for your past—celebrate your future.

I was literally just talking to myself right there.

Four Seasons Paris shoot with Mike Rosenthal—2018

CHAPTER TWO
KEEP IT CLASSY

S uccess in the hairstyling world relies entirely on repeat customers. I could work with every famous actress or model or musician and style for every magazine cover and fashion show in the universe, but if no one booked me a second time, my career would have ended long ago. I'm absolutely certain that the reason I continue to get called back isn't because I can create an updo better than anyone else—I mean, I think I'm a pretty great hairstylist, but there are plenty of great stylists out there. The reason I'm still working is because I have never forgotten that my job—even when it's fun and glamorous and I'm having a major pinch-me moment— is still a job, and it requires professionalism.

Maybe that sounds obvious, but the line between "personal" and "professional" can be hard to distinguish these days—especially on the gig economy side of things—and I've seen quite a few people sabotage their careers by not recognizing or respecting that line. I mean, we live in a world where sweats have become acceptable business attire and offices have Ping-Pong tables and video games. As a culture, we've embraced a 24/7 workweek and on-call lifestyle—and we document it all live and share it with the world. It can be confusing to know where the line is, and on which side of it you're standing.

Over the years I've become close friends with some of my clients—Chrissy Teigen, Khloé Kardashian, and Jessica Alba, to name a few—so I'm all for embracing friendship in the workplace and having fun. Enjoying your time at work means you're in the right gig. Social connections with colleagues and clients help keep you motivated, engaged, and focused. That said, when you're hired to do a job, don't forget that you're *working for someone*—not working your way to being friends with someone. You're there to help them with their brand or career. Respect, discretion, honesty, loyalty, a willingness to hustle, and an up-for-anything attitude are what will distinguish you from all the other talented people who are chasing the same dream.

PROFESSIONALISM NEVER GOES OUT OF STYLE

We've all heard it said that "good old-fashioned values" are a thing of the past. Headlines like "Millennials: The Me Me Me Generation" or articles describing the entire generation as "lazy and entitled" paint a pretty insulting picture. Of course, I know firsthand that those headlines don't tell the full story—I have a team of young assistants who bust their asses every day and make me proud in very high-profile, high-stakes environments. That said, coming of age in the era of social media, iPhones, and street-style casual every day has made it a bit tougher to remember some commonsense basics— things like eye contact (don't look at your phone while someone is talking to you!), privacy (not everything needs to be posted), and no overstepping boundaries on the job.

When I hire assistants to join my styling team, I try to be clear with my expectations: Set etiquette means respecting people's homes and spaces. That means use a coaster and no feet on the couch. Be yourself, but don't try to stand out in the wrong way (no crop tops or booty shorts, please). Let your client tell the stories—if you're hungover or you had a crazy weekend, keep it to yourself. (It's honestly amazing how many stylists come in and share stories about their sex lives or getting wasted and doing drugs. It's not a good look.) If your client is on the phone, don't talk and don't eavesdrop. Be conscious of the way your phone is facing so no one thinks you're taking a picture of them—or, even better, put your phone away.

Phone etiquette is important and complicated—it's become a real maze to navigate in the twenty-first century, especially if you're building a business on social media and you want to document and share content with your followers. The reality is that technology cuts both ways—it can launch you or ruin you. When I started out, the industry was so exclusive that in-demand Hollywood stylists could be rude and/or miserable to work with and still get hired, because no one could put them on blast on social. Oh, I have seen some shit. These days, we live in a world where everyone is watching all the time, and if you're a diva, word spreads fast. There's always someone who is not an asshole, someone who is respectful, talented, professional, and willing to work hard, waiting in the wings.

I recognize that it's easy to get caught up in the moment and want to capture content at the expense of excelling at your work or respecting the client or a coworker. I've seen it happen plenty. But please, resist the temptation. I remember one time a member of a glam squad posted from the set of a photo shoot for a celebrity ad campaign, not realizing that the partnership between the celebrity and the brand hadn't been announced publicly yet. Spilling the beans like that before an official announcement is not only bad form, it can jeopardize business deals or project launch dates, and put your career at risk.

Don't be that person.

Of course, professionalism looks different between industries. While I think it's pretty safe to assume that most workplaces prefer employees to show up on time and act respectfully and responsibly, the rules of etiquette might vary somewhat. But basics are basics: Dress appropriately and for the job you want. Act politely. Be engaged in the work when you're on the clock (that means no tweeting from the office). None of these guidelines seem that groundbreaking to me—most of them should be common sense. But I'm constantly floored by how often I hear of workers flaunting their hangovers or staring at their phones in meetings or complaining about assignments and missing deadlines. Self-awareness, keeping your shit together, and the ability to adapt to any situation without sacrificing class are the true signs of a professional.

LOOSE LIPS

t's a cliché that the salon breeds gossip (see *Steel Magnolias, Legally Blonde, Beauty Shop*), but it's also true. Working on the salon floor, and maybe even more so in a celebrity glam room, is the ultimate test—you might hear something from the person in your chair and be just *dying* to tell a friend, or you may hear a client bitching about someone and want more than anything to jump into the chatter. But whether it's gossiping *with* a client or *about* a client, it's a giant Don't. I totally understand the rush that comes from feeling like an insider, privy to information that others don't have. But I like to pretend as though I've signed an NDA* with every single person who sits in my chair. Most of the time I really have, but even in the cases where there is nothing formally binding me to secrecy, I act as if there is, because a professional relationship can end pretty quickly if you're perceived as a gossip. And a friend once told me that if someone is gossiping *to* you about other people, chances are they talk shit *about* you as well. A real zinger.

I'm *especially* careful not to join in conversations that

---

* *That's a nondisclosure agreement . . . basically a confidentiality contract saying I can't reveal anything I learn about the client while working with her. Break an NDA, and you might get fined or fired. Or, worse, get sued.*

a client might be having about someone else. Hollywood is a surprisingly small town, and I may know something about a deal or an event that my client and her agent are discussing, but I never chime in. It may seem like gossip is a way to bond with clients, but I always remember that the people in my chair—and the agent, manager, or publicist who represents them—have been in the business a long time. They may act friendly and interested when you offer a piece of inside info, but, believe me, in the back of their minds they're taking note: this person can't be trusted, we shouldn't work with them again. Some of my relationships and friendships with clients and their teams go back ten years, and that trusted bond is worth more than toilet paper in quarantine.

The relationship between a client and a hairstylist is a surprisingly intimate one. We're in your home or in your face, sometimes for a long time. Even when I'm just doing an easy updo, I'm with someone for two or two and a half hours. If I'm working on a commercial, it can be more like a twelve-hour day. In that time, clients take business meetings about deals they're considering, or they might pitch partnership ideas over the phone. I've heard things that could easily make the cover of *People* or go viral on the *Daily Mail* in an instant. Before celebrities could tell their own stories on Instagram, I knew people—not just hairstylists but makeup artists or wardrobe people or celebrity assistants—who would sell stories about their clients to make money, and I always thought that was so gross. Before the days of iPhones, stylists or salons would also call the paps on their clients. (We had a receptionist or two at the salon where I worked who were fired for that very thing.)

I find much more satisfaction in being considered a trust-worthy person than I ever would in delivering a piece of gossip that will dominate the headlines for twenty-four hours before lining tomorrow's trash cans. Even a juicy tidbit that seems small and unimportant—so-and-so has six toes!—I keep it to myself.*

My point is this: whether you're working with a person who lives in the public eye or just a regular private person, try to remember that everyone is a human being with feelings. This really is a life lesson as much as it is good business etiquette. The fact that I never called the paparazzi or served as a "source" for celebrity gossip doesn't exactly make me a hero. I'm just a decent person who respects the people I work for, and respects their personal lives. I see how hard they work, and how much they give up. Their lives are fabulous but also challenging, because money and fame make things complicated. Having your clients' backs and understanding what is private without them having to spell it out for you really is a job requirement, and that's true in pretty much any profession. The world is small, and individual industries are smaller. You never know who used to work together, or who went to college together, or who used to date and are still friends. Once you're branded a gossip, that reputation will follow you, and I promise, it's not worth sabotaging a relationship, or your entire career, for a few moments of feeling cool.

As I tell my assistants, loose lips sink ships. Let your clients dish if they want, but respond by nodding your head,

---

* *OMG, I actually do know someone with six toes, but you'll never find out who!!!*

not opening your mouth. Just because someone needs to get something off their chest doesn't mean you need to get involved and add fuel to the fire.*

Discretion is self-preservation. Challenge yourself to disengage from the chatter—I guarantee you'll feel better about yourself and the world when you stop shit-talking other people. I have a friend who has made it her goal this year to stop gossiping, and she's really inspired me to steer clear of tempting chats. If you're up for the challenge, maybe get your friends and coworkers involved and make a conscious effort to say something nice or nothing at all. There's something in Scripture about this somewhere . . . but I was too busy gossiping in church to remember it.

HONESTY IS THE BEST POLICY

Of all the career insights I hope to impart through this book, the one I feel most confident applies to every single person in every single industry is this: business is about relationships. Making connections, developing rapport, forging bonds, creating mutual respect—this is how careers move forward and new opportunities are created. It seems almost silly to mention the importance of qualities like honesty and loyalty in building strong relationships,

---

* *Also, studies show that when you gossip about someone else, people associate YOU with those bad traits. It's called "spontaneous trait transference," and it means that the more you complain about one colleague's arrogance or another's idiocy, the more likely it is that others will consider you an arrogant idiot. Something to keep in mind!*

because obviously. But in the quest to get to the next rung of the ladder, it can be easy to overlook these very elementary, but increasingly vital, aspects of connecting. People succeed in groups, so you don't want to piss off yours.

Honesty takes many forms, and in my industry, it can be surprisingly hard to come by. This is because it's difficult to tell a client something they may not want to hear, and also because when you're more focused on getting ahead than getting along, you can talk yourself into making some really bad decisions. Some dishonesty is black and white, like skimming money off the top or double billing or taking packages of swag that were actually sent for someone else. In other industries, it might look more like stealing someone else's idea or taking credit for their work (the '80s classic *Working Girl* comes to mind). Keeping tips that you were supposed to split, snagging client leads that were meant to be shared, or sabotaging a coworker's big opportunity . . . it all fits the bill. There's no gray area in those scenarios, no way to trick yourself into thinking you're not doing anything wrong. And yet I've seen these things happen—not because anyone started out intending to cheat and steal, but because someone got blinded by the lure of the dollar or the fabulous lifestyle and figured their client was so wealthy that nobody would ever notice.

But there's also a blurrier form of dishonesty, a trap that well-intentioned people find themselves in when they work in the world of celebrities and influencers, and that is the trap of becoming a yes-man. Once stars reach a certain level of fame, they often find themselves surrounded by yes-people. *Should I do this partnership deal?* Yes! *Does this job offer seem on-brand for me?* Of course! *Is this relationship good for me?* Totally!

Yes-people aren't usually trying to be dishonest. They're trying to tell a client what they want to hear, because they want to get paid, or they want to get hired back, or they want to make the person happy and they think they're being respectful. Oh, and also: they want whichever fabulous, famous person they're working with to *like* them. But what the yes-men (or yes-women) don't realize is that as long as you're coming from a place of wanting to help, and as long as that intention is clear in your delivery, what people want to hear is the truth. There is a way to be honest while still being polite and respectful and kind, and if a client asks me for advice, I'm always ready with an honest opinion, whether it's to say that, no, maybe bangs aren't the best look for you, or, yes, you probably should break up with him or her, or no, don't tweet that. My real talk always comes from a place of wanting the best for the people around me, and I've learned that my clients really appreciate that, especially the people who, as their star rises, find themselves surrounded by more and more yes-men. Relationships get complicated once folks are on your payroll.

You don't have to work with celebrities or even work in a service industry to find yourself falling into the yes-man trap. I've seen employees agree with everything their bosses say because they want to be liked or they want a promotion, or because they think that agreeing with a supervisor is what they're paid to do. But always remember that no matter your job, you were hired because your smarts and your opinions are valuable. A good boss will appreciate respectful disagreement, especially if it's in the interest of the company as a whole. Good employers want their teams to make smart decisions and succeed—they don't just want to dictate and be "yessed" all day. And if you do have a boss who's a dictator? See page 23 on risk-taking, and get the hell out of there.

ATTITUDE OF GRATITUDE

I s there anything classier than a proper thank-you? I honestly don't know that there is. Showing gratitude, whether it's to someone who held a door for you or to the employer who gave you a job, is a way of honoring other people's contributions and acknowledging that we are all in this together. No one succeeds, or even survives, without help and support. It is also, according to Emily Post, Etiquette 101.

Of course I've always known, at least abstractly, that being grateful is good for your career and your heart and your soul. If I learned anything from my Bible-studying days, it was that gratitude is one of the most important qualities a person can embody. As an extra bonus, being grateful—and focusing on gratitude—makes you feel better about what you do have and less envious when others have something you don't. Guys, being grateful actually promotes psychological and emotional healing. Science! Imagine being content with what you have and not obsessed with wanting more, more, more. Sounds dreamy, right?

Cultivating an attitude of gratitude takes practice. It's easy to focus on what you're grateful for every now and then—at Thanksgiving, maybe, or when you're suddenly

faced with a hard time or something unexpectedly wonderful happens—but if you're mindlessly going about your
daily routine, it can be hard to remember to take stock of the
small pleasures or to appreciate the luxuries you usually
take for granted. But if quarantine has taught us anything,
it is to appreciate the little things in life. Your morning
coffee. A friendly neighbor. Entire TikTok feeds devoted
to dog content. I've found that a gratitude journal, in which
I write down three things I'm grateful for at the end of
each day, helps keep gratitude front of mind. Sometimes I
write down the big stuff—my husband, Mike; my health;
the fact that we have a safe place to call home—but sometimes it's a really good Rice Krispies Treat, or the fact that
a friend fostered a puppy.

Research shows that people who practice gratitude are
happier and more satisfied with their lives, but that's really what it is . . . a practice. The more you practice taking
stock of everything you have to be thankful for and writing some of those things down, the better you'll get at iden-
tifying the small opportunities for gratitude as they arise.
Seriously, whenever I'm on a good stretch of keeping my
gratitude journal, I start looking at my whole life through
the lens of gratitude. And once you're paying attention,
you'll notice that plenty more than three opportunities to
say thank you come up each day. I also keep a full gratitude
list in my phone. It's just a simple list of twenty things I'm
grateful for, and I look at it whenever life feels hard or
stressful or overwhelming. I also keep a list of everything
I'm grateful for about myself. That one can feel harder to
fill, but it's so important to document. It's too easy to fall
into the trap of negative self-talk, so a visual reminder

of all the reasons we're awesome can come in real handy when we need a moment of self-compassion.

All that said, gratitude *isn't* just an attitude. It can be an action—and a really rewarding one, too. I find it incredibly gratifying when someone takes a moment to thank me for my work, or for an opportunity— I always remember those people. (And let's be real: assistants who say thank you are getting booked more often than ones who don't.) And I know I'm far from alone here. Back in 2010, when I was working for John Galliano at the Dior shows, I'll never forget a certain fresh face on the runway scene bringing handwritten thank-you notes backstage at every show she walked to thank John for making her dreams come true. That polite kid's name was Karlie Kloss. I know that her gesture meant so much to him, and I remember thinking to myself, *Wow. That is really fucking classy.* I mean, how often, especially these days, do people take the time to write a proper thank-you note, let alone multiple thank-you notes to the same person? There's a reason why Karlie has had such a long and successful career.

Khloé Kardashian is another example of a superstar who never misses an opportunity to say thank you or write a card or send a nice email. It means a lot, and whenever I receive one of her cute notes it's a great reminder for me to follow her lead. Because even the most well-intentioned of us can get caught up in the day-to-day and forget to take a moment to acknowledge the contributions of others. But we all know how good it feels to be recognized for our hard work, so why not pay that forward? It takes so little time and so little effort, and it is so meaningful to someone else.

It should go without saying that you should always,

always send a thank-you note after an interview—or, at the very least, a thank-you email. Thank mentors who took the time to have lunch with you. Thank clients for trusting you, not just when the contract is signed, but often and sincerely as you work with them. Thank the people in your company who make your life a little bit easier. There is never a wrong time to say thank you, or a wrong person to thank.

When it comes to sending tokens of gratitude, the most meaningful gifts come down to knowing your audience. Personally, I hate getting flowers. They're beautiful, of course, and the gesture is thoughtful and always appreciated . . . but I'm usually not home long enough to really enjoy those pricey arrangements, and they inevitably end up in the trash. It just strikes me as a waste of money. The token of gratitude I appreciate more than anything is a donation in my name to a cause that's important to me, like an animal rights group, the ACLU, or a nonprofit that helps underserved communities. Every time I get a flower delivery, I can't help but think of the good that could have been done with that money. So get creative. Postmate a colleague who helped you out with a big presentation some ice cream or their favorite lunch or an afternoon caffeine fix. Offer to watch a friend's kid for an hour. Send someone a Cameo! (The entire *Cheer* squad is on there, just saying.) These little gestures of appreciation go a long way. Oh, btw, can you DM me with your thoughtful gift ideas? THANK YOU!

Daily Front Row Awards, where I received my award from the one and only Kris Jenner—2018

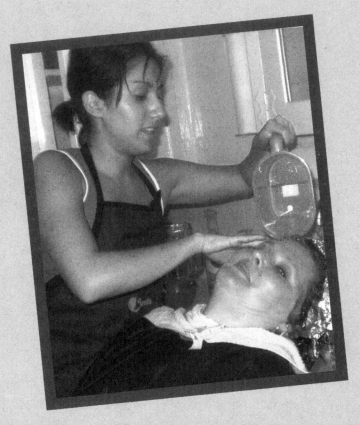

Using my mom as my hair school model—2004

CHAPTER THREE
DON'T LET
THE INTERNET
RUSH YOU

ocial media is an incredible source of inspiration—
you can go behind the scenes of whatever career
interests you and get a firsthand look at people you
admire. Envisioning your own rise to success is a lot easier
once you have some idea of what it takes and you've seen
someone else do it. All those closed-door industries—most
of which have a long history of being discriminatory—
suddenly seem penetrable, and the mysteries of *How do I
get a foot in the door?* or *What does that job actually look
like?* are revealed. It can be just the kick in the pants you
need to go out, fight for what you deserve, and conquer the
world.

But.

Even when the action in your feed inspires you to do
all the things and do them now, the truth will always be
that nothing happens overnight. I know it might seem like
those accounts you follow appeared out of thin air, scoring
invitations to inspiring conferences or big endorsements

or partnerships the minute they arrived on the scene, but I can assure you that, 99.9 percent of the time, the people behind those accounts have put in the work. Probably for years. It takes time—usually a pretty long time—to get from A to Z, and that reality can get lost in the deluge of highly curated Stories, Tweets, TikToks, and Snaps.

DON'T LET THE FILTERS FOOL YOU

It can be tempting to see other people's careers take off and start to feel like the universe owes you the same. I know it's frustrating and unfair, but entitlement isn't a good look on anyone. You aren't owed success just because someone else is doing well. In fact, an attitude of entitlement is an easy way to sabotage any success you might already have. Think about it—we've all come across people who are hurting or angry or jealous because they believe that they're entitled to what everyone else has. How often do you want to jump on a project with that person, or go on a work trip with them? Never? Me too, trust me.

The reality is that this lens through which we all admire (or envy) one another is pretty distorted. Instagram is not an unfiltered look at people's lives. Twitter is not a documentation of everyone's innermost thoughts. People are showing you their best days, their wittiest jokes. It's easy to project confidence when you have 100 filters and a ring light at your disposal, but no one has a perfect life. Not even the celebrities walking the red carpets or influencers going on glamorous work trips. It takes a lot of effort to get those glossy pics, and those influencers are working hard AF to create constant content. We're talking dragging umbrellas, drinks, and fruit platters to the rocky beach at 5:00 a.m. for good light. So don't be fooled. All the people you're following are working hard to make their lives look so perfect, and they're all battling their own demons and insecurities. Nobody is happy all of the time. We're all human beings having a human experience on the same planet. It's just that now we have technology that allows us to make everything appear beautiful and effortless.

I often wonder what would happen if you were to hook yourself up to a heart monitor while scrolling through Instagram. You think you're happy in the moment, but then you come away feeling down, because it's really hard to scroll for an hour and think afterward, *I'm super-thrilled with where I am in my life!* Plenty of studies link excessive social media use to increased anxiety, which should surprise no one. Getting caught up in comparing yourself to the accounts in your feed can be isolating and polarizing, and you have to be sure not to fall into the trap of seeing other people's accomplishments as a measure of your own success, because most of the time you don't know what's going on behind the screens. (See what I did there?) And you aren't seeing the years of work that got them all those followers or scored them all those invites.

Social media as we know it only really took off about ten years ago, so it's a common misconception that the biggest-name influencers didn't get started until then, either. I've seen this myth take hold even among my assistants, who sometimes wonder aloud if a new-to-them hairstylist just appeared out of thin air. After years of working with me and hearing my story, they should know better, but that's how easy it is to believe that what you see in your feed is the whole story. A lot of today's most successful influencers were early adopters on Blogspot and started creating content and building their communities long before the advent of social media. What's been especially inspiring to watch is how many different genres of influencers are now given opportunities, and I hope that continues to flourish.

Similarly, a lot of people are skeptical of celebrities who've launched successful brands and products—and, yes, there are more and more of them these days. But questioning their success is crazy to me. Does having a famous name help a business get off the ground? Sure. But if you think Jessica Alba woke up one day and launched the Honest Company on a whim, think again. And if you believe people are going to continue paying their hard-earned money for a product that doesn't deliver, just because a famous face is on it, well, that's also incorrect. There have been plenty of celeb-backed product lines that flopped; you've just probably never heard of them. (Because, you know, they flopped.) If there's one thing that working behind the scenes with entertainment and beauty legends like Jennifer Lopez or Cindy Crawford has taught me, it is that *these ladies work their asses off.* They are not handed their success just because they're gorgeous and crazy talented. They have passion and dedication to what they do, they are professional, and they put in a lot of years paying their dues. They're also managing many time-consuming and unseen responsibilities that most of us don't have to think about, because with success comes more and more people who are relying on that success to continue. And some are managing multiple careers and families! They're singing or acting or modeling, and then they're also overseeing a business and all of the people and services and products that are a part of that business. That's no small thing. Maybe you're thinking, *Oh, poor them, nice problem to have.* And that's easy to say from the outside looking in. But notoriety and success aren't cure-alls, and they don't magically make life easier.

I'm not trying to be a buzzkill. I know it's fun to day-dream about becoming the Next Big Thing. And the path to success really is shorter today than it once was, thanks to the speed of communication in the digital world and the access and exposure offered by social media and ecomm. But I still think it's important to manage your expectations. The next time you're tempted to grumble about that per-son who seems to have hit it big overnight or whose path is easier than yours because they're famous, try to remember that success rarely favors the passive or lazy, and it is very, very rarely instantaneous.

You could say I'm a prime example of this. Plenty of people think my career didn't begin until I launched my Instagram account in 2010. I'm pretty sure some of them even believe that the Kardashians "discovered" me out of nowhere, as if I wasn't busting my ass for a decade before that. And honestly, had one of my celeb clients discovered me hiding in a salon somewhere, that would have been GREAT. I could have saved myself years of sleep depri-vation, and I could have gone to all the birthday parties and baby showers and family holidays I missed when I was working myself ragged. The reality is that in my early salon days, when I was a manager at the Hollywood hot spot Estilo, I wanted to get my cosmetology license, but the big hair schools like Vidal Sassoon and Toni & Guy cost nearly twenty grand—a little out of my price range, given that I could barely cover my rent each month. So in 2004 I enrolled in a state-funded cosmetology program in downtown L.A. and went to class in the morning, spent afternoons working in any salon that would have me in order to get the hours required for my license, and worked nights as a restaurant hostess. Those were the days when I really learned the art of the hustle.*

After that, I spent another year assisting at The Chris McMillan Salon. Chris, who's one of the most famous celebrity hairstylists of all time (he does Jennifer Aniston's hair—you've probably heard of her?), was a stylist at Estilo but eventually opened his own shop, and I was thrilled to get on the payroll there . . . even if it meant more assisting. It wasn't until 2007 that I went out on my own, working twelve-hour days behind the chair in order to build my clientele. And let me tell you, going on my own was really scary. I had to cross my fingers and hope that all the clients I'd been shampooing and blow-drying and feeding meters for would support me. And plenty of them did, but those early days were slow, and I second-guessed everything: *Was this a mistake? Should I have relied on the steady paycheck and the comfort of tips I earned while assisting?* I spent a good year in the salon just getting myself settled, praying the right publicist would come in for a blowout.

---

* *And, also, the Art of Flirting with Italian Bartenders, but my husband's reading this.*

All those people who think my career *started* when Instagram took off are discounting a full decade I spent finding my way through L.A., sweeping and cutting and curling and blow-drying until my fingers ached, taking classes, and shamelessly networking as much as humanly possible so that I could make a name for myself. The point is, don't fool yourself into thinking success comes quickly. And don't put arbitrary deadlines on yourself to hit each milestone in a certain amount of time or by a certain age. Overnight sensations aren't real, and hopefully understanding that will relieve some of the pressure. All you can do is put one foot in front of the other. As long as you're making strides toward your goal, whatever that may be, don't get frustrated about how long it's taking. It takes *everyone* a while, but most people don't post about the slog because it's more interesting to share the milestones than the grunt work. The good news, though, is that there's still plenty of time. I really hope you hear that. No matter how old you are right now, YOU STILL HAVE SO MUCH TIME to make yourself into whatever you want to be. You may even change your mind about what you want to be along the way, and THAT'S OKAY, TOO. Don't get discouraged by the inner expectations you put on yourself, or the outer expectations it can feel like social media and society put on you.

And in case you're reading this and thinking of that one person you know whose random tweet or TikTok immediately went viral, please remember that viral "fame" is usually fleeting. The people I've known who found success really quickly also lost it really quickly. For the kind of career that endures, there is no shortcut. Focus on working hard and developing your talents without buckling under the pressure to keep up with the Joneses, and remember that nothing good comes easily.

THE HUSTLE IS REAL

I get so many DMs from people who feel discouraged because things aren't happening for them as quickly as they'd expected. My advice to these people is always the same: keep waking up and showing up. I know it might seem like my career was one big break after another, but the reality is that in between those major moments were months and years of monotony. It was like *Groundhog Day*, getting up and going to the salon and cutting or washing or blow-drying sometimes difficult clients' hair and coming home and getting up and going to the salon and working on sometimes hard-to-please clients' kids' hair and coming home, and on and on, day in and day out.

As with many industries, being low on the food chain also meant occasionally enduring a kind of casual abuse from my superiors. I worked for one old-school stylist who wanted me to pay attention to him at all times. If my gaze left the foils when we were coloring a client's hair, he would paint the bleach on my fingers. Bleach! On my fingers! That certainly snapped me back to attention. Of course, this isn't just a glam industry issue. I've heard plenty of *Devil Wears Prada* stories from friends in every industry—getting calls from bosses at all hours, being told to lie to higher-ups when a boss screws up. There are Miranda Priestlys everywhere.

In the hair world, being an assistant also means working seven days a week, because you're not just helping with the actual cutting and styling, you're also prepping everything beforehand and cleaning up afterward. You're the first person in and the last one out, and, I'll be honest, it's a grind even in the most glamorous gigs. I'll never forget working at Paris Fashion Week, prepping wigs for the Louis Vuitton show until 1:00 a.m. and then going home for a brief nap only to return for call time at 5:00 a.m. My fingers were literally bleeding from sewing wigs, and my hands were covered in calluses. Then I'd rush to a hotel to style an actress who was sitting to watch the show and then move to the next show and do it all over again. It's an incredible learning experience, but it can be brutal; anyone who joins this line of work because they think it will be champagne-toasting fun is in for a rude awakening.*

I'm not suggesting that putting in the time is synonymous with running yourself into the ground—burnout is real, and you don't want to derail your career before it even takes off. Looking back now, I know I could have slowed down a bit throughout those early years and still gotten to where I am today. But I do want to be realistic about what the hustle can look and feel like, and the fact that no matter what your goal, you have to put in your time. I made it through those particularly hard years because I saw the sacrifice for what it was: an investment in myself and my future.

---

* *I only made it through a few fashion seasons doing this, but there are some talented hairstylists who assist for years on fashion shows. Major props.*

After I went out on my own, I needed to remind myself of all this constantly. Being your own boss is tricky—you're either working so hard that you have no time for yourself and you're constantly exhausted and frustrated, or you're not as busy as you want to be and you're constantly worried the work won't come and you're never going to make it. When I would lose a job to someone else or get a cancellation at the last minute, both of which meant I wasn't getting paid, I really struggled to keep my eye on the prize. I call it the freelance blues, and when you're in the thick of it, it can feel like a no-win situation.

When Mike and I had been dating for about three years, he found himself having a slow year, career-wise. He's a photographer, so for him, as for me, the work can ebb and flow. It can feel like you're either running around nonstop or standing around waiting for the phone to ring— somehow it's rarely anything in between. And Mike's not just any photographer, he's uber-talented and successful and, sure, maybe I'm biased, but this is a guy who does editorial shoots for the biggest magazines, and commercials and campaigns with the most in-demand celebrities and brands in the world. You may even know him from his days as a judge and photographer on *America's Next Top Model* (season 11!). What I'm saying is, he's the real deal.*

But everyone has to ride out the slow seasons, and during this particular year Mike was starting to question himself. He was going through one of those periods when you start to wonder if you're wasting your time, and the next thing

* *He's also really humble, so surely this page will embarrass him.*

you know, you start to doubt your abilities, and that is a very slippery slope. It was painful for me to watch, not just because I love him but because I know how talented he is and how hard he works, and I could empathize with what he was going through. He struggled for close to a year. My advice to him was the same as what I offer to those discouraged people in my DMs: You have to keep going. You are too talented to give up. Together we brainstormed ways he could network and meet publicists who might send him new clients, and things started to pick up again. Now he has more work than he knows what to do with, and plenty of Mike Rosenthal stans. (The real ones recognize his work on the Kylie Lip Kit boxes!)

Investing in yourself is vital—whether that means paying for training or spending time networking or waiting out the slow periods—and the reward on the other side will be worth it. Paying your dues looks different depending on your career path, but the hustle is real no matter what industry you're in. The assistants on my team who get ahead are not the ones who expect promotions or complain about wanting to do more interesting things. They're the ones who are eager to pitch in, aren't above doing even the most menial task, have a great attitude, and are dependable. As a boss, I promote people who have made themselves indispensable through their actions rather than their words and who never bring up problems without offering solutions.

In all this talk about getting ahead, I just want to reiterate that the work doesn't go away the minute you "make it." There is no finish line. We all make the mistake of thinking that once you get that job or promotion or hit a major work goal, your life will be happier and easier. In reality, your responsibilities may change—you might be able to delegate more, or make the decisions rather than follow orders—but after putting in the work to build and grow a career or a brand, it doesn't just stop. Now you have to take care of this baby that you raised. And you've got employees who rely on you to lead and guide them. As long as you want it all to be working, you're really going to be working. And working and working.

RACK UP THOSE CONTACTS

There's one major upside to paying your dues and climbing the ladder over a period of years rather than months. When you stay in an industry long enough, you see the same faces over and over—the assistant becomes the top publicist becomes the head of a hot new PR firm. The extra becomes the series regular becomes the Oscar nominee. The receptionist becomes the salon hairstylist becomes the hair-care line founder. You see where I'm going. When I think back to 2010, the kids just starting out were me, Mary Phillips, queen of perfect makeup, and Karla Welch, one of the biggest names in celebrity wardrobe styling today. Over the past decade our careers have evolved pretty dramatically, and along the way we've helped each other up by working together or sending each other business or talking one another up in the press. Success for one of us has been success for all of us.

Over more than a decade of working, I met people from

all walks of life, and in every different industry. Making those connections, and always behaving with grace and professionalism (even if some early Facebook party pics might seem to say different), meant that I had a pretty deep Rolodex by the time I wanted to launch a business. I had so many questions, so many ideas I wanted to run by people who knew what they were talking about, and all those years of building my professional network paid off big-time. Asking someone if you can "pick their brain" means requesting that they spare their valuable time and share their hard-earned knowledge. It's not a request I make lightly, but when I asked A.L.C. designer Andrea Lieberman or Huda Kattan of Huda Beauty or makeup mogul Sonia Kashuk for advice, they were thrilled to share their wisdom, and I believe that was because they'd seen me showing up, day after day, for years. They knew my work ethic. And good thing they did, because their insight saved me time and saved me money and probably saved me from many, many mistakes.

THE WORK BEHIND THE WORK

Here's a secret I might as well tell you now: the more success you find in any type of work, the less time you actually have to do that work. This isn't bad, necessarily, but it's an important thing to understand as you navigate your career and decide how high you really want to climb.

Think about a chef. Maybe she starts out as a prep cook. Over the years she'll work her way up the ranks, getting promoted to line cook and maybe sous-chef. During that time, she's really *in* the work, creating new dishes and honing her knife skills and experimenting with new ingredients. But as her star rises, she may become an executive chef or decide to open up her own restaurant. Now she has to meet with investors and hire a staff and maybe even work the front of house. The more important she becomes in the culinary world, and the more her name becomes a brand, the less time she'll have to actually make food. To do the thing she was passionate about in the first place.

This is a reality across industries, and I point it out because when people talk about the hustle and putting in the work, I think they forget sometimes that as your career grows you have to get schooled in so many areas outside of the field you started in. I showcase my hairstyles and hair products on Insta because that's my brand, but knowing how to cut and style and braid with the best of them isn't enough anymore. The skills outside of hairstyling that I've had to learn in the last decade include: how to scale a business, how to find the right representation, how to understand social media algorithms, how to navigate bookkeeping and taxes (hairstylists are notorious for getting audited), how to take good photos and tag the right brands for maximum exposure, how to create a brand message, what to look for in an aerosol lab, how to pitch investors or interview formulators of quality hair products, and what the hell EBITDA is. I had to figure out what to ask at different fragrance houses or distribution centers, what makes a good advertising or marketing campaign, how to create training materials for employees, how to present to retailers, and how to write copy for the website and the products. Most recently, I had to learn how to manage an entire team working remotely while we all navigated the impact of a global pandemic on our professional and personal lives. Even delegating the work takes work—interviewing publicists and managers and web developers and account managers. None of these are duties I thought I would need to know back when I was in Utah or when I was in beauty school or when I was assisting famous stylists. I didn't even understand that these types of responsibilities existed.

The million-dollar question: How did I learn to do any of these things? Sometimes I learned by doing or by watching others who created successful brands across all different industries. And plenty of times I figured it out by reading books (so many books!) on airplanes while flying from one job to another. But most of the time it was from LISTENING and PAYING ATTENTION and not acting like I already knew what I didn't.

And listen, I'm not saying it isn't any fun to do this work. The rush I get from the business work is different from the one I get from hairstyling, but it's a rush nonetheless. Coming up with brand names and product names and innovative modern packaging is creative in its own right, and I get a lot of satisfaction from that work, because it's super-rewarding to build a company that reflects your values. But it's not the same creative high I get from seeing one of my hairstyles go down the red carpet.

Point is, there is a lot of work behind the work that the internet will not show you, so I want you to go in with *eyessss wide open*. And now I hear that Train song in my head. Ugh.

IT'S OKAY TO NOT WANT THE CHAOS

One of my favorite assistants, Alex, moved to L.A. from Chicago and hit the ground running. She was organized and talented and worked hard—my clients loved her, and I was like a proud mama bear. So you can imagine my surprise when, after about two years together, she wrote me an email explaining that while she was grateful for the experience and had learned a lot, she'd decided the celebrity styling world wasn't for her. One of the things she realized while working for me was that she didn't want to get into the politics of the L.A. hustle. That just wasn't her definition of success. I think her exact words were "Don't take this the wrong way, but I don't want your life." Instead she wanted to be a big fish in a small(er) pond, have a less chaotic career, and really kill it in the Chicago hair scene. She was in touch with what would make her happy, and she wasn't swayed by what might have seemed like the more fabulous choice. I can't tell you how much I respected that. A couple of years later, another one of my assistants, Derek, made the same decision and moved to Nashville. I was so proud of both of them, and even more than being proud, I was impressed by their self-possession and maturity.

Figuring out what success means to you is the most critical element of creating an awesome life. For some people, the measure is fame or fortune or followers. But studies show that for more and more people, the definition of success lies in the intangibles: the freedom to make your own schedule, the ability to work from anywhere in the world, the satisfaction of doing work that feels meaningful even if it isn't super-lucrative. Success might mean having fulfilling relationships, or just simply feeling happy. So before you dive into the hustler life, take a step back and ask the bigger question: *What does success look like for me? When I dream of my best life, what am I doing? If money didn't matter, what would I be doing every day?*

Understanding the answers to these questions will give you clarity and guidance in your professional endeavors and your personal ones. Think about your proudest (not necessarily your biggest) achievements, your happiest memories, your greatest fears. You might even have to jot these down on a piece of paper and do some detective work. If your proudest achievements have nothing to do with money but instead are about helping others . . . well, that's a hint. If the thought of going into an office every day makes your stomach drop, maybe the C suite isn't for you. If your happiest memories involve being surrounded by people, perhaps working from home isn't actually your dream.

There is no right answer to these questions, and your definition might not match up with your colleague's or best friend's. But figuring that out early will save you the pain that comes from achieving someone else's version of success and realizing that you aren't happy. Had I stuck to the definition of success that my parents taught me, I'd be living in Utah and raising four kids right about now. And there's nothing wrong with that for someone else, but it's not what I wanted.

It's also entirely possible that your definition of success will change over time. You may think you know exactly what you want to do with your career, and you may start following that dream, and you may realize along the way that . . . wait . . . maybe this *isn't* the life you want after all. THAT'S OKAY, TOO. You won't know unless you try, but once you do, if you realize that it's not making you happy? Don't force yourself to power through because you think you should. You have nothing to prove, and there are a million different ways to be happy and successful. I'm not condoning giving up when something is hard, which is certainly not what those assistants did. I'm saying that if your gut is telling you something isn't right, and there are just too many trade-offs you can't abide, it's okay to rethink your plan, both professionally and personally. Make sure your life is reflecting your values and ambitions.

Sometimes, though, those thoughts of bailing come when things are getting tough, and instead of keeping your nose to the grindstone you may be tempted to check out. One truth I know for sure is that something will always come up. If you're looking for an excuse *not* to pursue your dreams, you'll find it. It's a normal impulse, but in moments like that, you have to get honest with yourself: Is this really not what you want? Or are you just feeling scared and insecure and exhausted?

I should point out that both Alex and Derek have gone on to great success in their respective cities. It's not like they gave up on their dreams; their dreams just evolved. I've also had former assistants who stayed in L.A. and have thriving careers.

There's a flip side to all of this, and that's when you *do* know what you want, but the internet makes you feel like you're supposed to want something different. As soon as I got into hairstyling, my career ambitions were to grow my business and earn respect within the industry. But as I found success working with celebrities, the reality TV offers started pouring in. That wasn't necessarily something I wanted for my career, and I had to remind myself of that when opportunities came up that on paper seemed irresistible but in reality would *not* have made me happy. It was especially difficult to navigate these kinds of offers because I couldn't find many people whose careers I wanted to emulate—people who were doing glam and building brands and also creating killer content. That wasn't a career model that had taken off yet. It would have been easy to point to the Rachel Zoes and Brad Goreskis of the world and say, "Those are the most successful glam names, I want what they have!" They've both achieved so much and are incredibly talented. But at the end of the day, I had to be honest and admit to myself that my ambitions, and my personality, were different. I had to create a path that would make me happy. Also, I swear way too much to be on a TV show.

I know what you're thinking: *But she posts a ton of selfies on social media. How "behind the scenes" does she really want to be?* Please understand that it's very easy to live your life on Instagram and forget that anyone is paying attention. That's comfortable for me. It's when a *New York Times* profile calls me the "Most Influential Hairstylist in the World"* or a magazine feature comes out that I have the *oh-shit-people-are-watching* moments. Plus, I feel weird about getting credit for concepts or new products or companies that a lot of people helped me create. When I was offered the cover of

---

* *Yes, that happened, and it blew my mind and still feels completely surreal.*

Women's Wear Daily, I freaked out a little. It was an honor, for sure, but when the magazine pitched featuring me alone on the cover, it didn't feel right. In the end, I was able to get a group of OUAI and Mane Addicts employees, my assistants, and some social influencers who had supported both brands to join me for the photo shoot, and *that* felt right. That felt awesome, actually. I am acutely aware that I'm not the center of the universe, and that my success is shared with the people on my teams and in my community.

The internet might make you feel like you need to be bigger and shinier, and it might make you think you should want more, but there is so much to be said for knowing what you want to do and doing it well. Let me remind you of a truth that should be obvious but gets lost sometimes: you should be doing what makes you happy, not just what gets you more followers, or more fame, or even more money. I know that hairstyling makes me happy because I can picture myself doing it in my seventies. But I tell everyone who starts out in the business the same thing, and I think this applies to a lot of jobs: you have to really love it, because otherwise the blood, sweat, and tears just won't be worth it. I hope we normalize figuring out what you want, changing your goals, and learning to love yourself through the process.

ONE PART PATIENCE, TWO PARTS LUCK

It's time I tell you the story of how I scored my very first job in the hair industry. Picture this: Culver City Starbucks, 2001. I'm wearing my favorite low-cut Blue Cult bell-bottom jeans and a bandeau top (my outfits were all very *Lizzie McGuire*–inspired back then), and I'm sipping a Tazoberry Tea while interviewing for some sort of secretary gig that I saw posted on Craigslist. The woman sitting at the table next to me, clearly within earshot, casually observes the whole exchange and, after the person interviewing me leaves, says hello to me and strikes up a conversation. It turns out that she works at Estilo, one of the trendiest salons in the city, and happens to be on the hunt for a new receptionist. I don't know what I said in that interview that caught her ear, or if I looked the part, or if she just got a good vibe from me, but she offered me the position on the spot. Talk about luck. I'm not willing to say that I wouldn't be where I am today if that woman and I hadn't been in the same place at the same time, because, who knows. But sitting in that specific seat in that specific Starbucks on that specific day really did change my life.

Later, when I first started styling on my own at The Chris McMillan Salon, a client I'd never met before needed a blow-dry, and I was the only one available. It was the dreaded 7:00 p.m. slot, when the salon is about to close, but I said yes and went about my work. Her name was Amanda and she was perfectly nice, though we didn't really talk much. Still, I gave her a great blowout, and she was happy enough with my work that she requested me for subsequent appointments. Over time, I realized that she was a celebrity publicist. About six months into doing her hair, someone at the salon told me that she wasn't just any publicist—she was Amanda Silverman of 42 West, a high-profile entertainment PR firm, and she represented people like Rihanna and Pharrell Williams and Charlize Theron. (She now has her own firm, The Lede, and is an even bigger deal and is helping me with PR for this very book!) This was during the pre-Instagram era, when stylists could only rely on publicists to get their names to celebrities. Still, I didn't ask her for any favors or try to take advantage of the relationship; I just kept my head down and did my job. Eventually she told the other publicists at her office that a girl at Chris McMillan was really good at blowouts, and that's how I ended up working with Sofia Vergara and Christina Hendricks, back when *Modern Family* and *Mad Men* were still new. I finally had my shot at blowing my way to the top.

In both instances, luck obviously played a major role. But it wasn't *all* luck—I was lucky that Estilo's hiring manager sat next to me, but if she didn't like what she overheard, she never would have offered me a job. And I was lucky to have that publicist end up in my chair, but if she wasn't impressed with my work or my demeanor, she wouldn't have recommended me to her clients. Still, I am the first person to acknowledge that luck contributed to these opportunities presenting themselves—and patience played a huge role in creating that luck. If I'd been constantly trying to force my way into the next thing rather than allowing time for opportunities to develop, I would have missed so many opportunities like these. Not everyone you encounter will become a fairy godmother, but if you put in the work for long enough, and you're not an a-hole or a diva and you act professionally and with kindness, you never know who might give you your next big break.

Patience can be really hard to come by when the internet

is telling you to hurry it up or that you're not good enough. But figuring out how to be patient has served me both practically—when clients are always running late, what other choice do you have?—and in the more big-picture career sense. When I was getting my cosmetology license and sweeping floors every afternoon, all I wanted was to be able to do hair, but I had to wait. And then I was watching stylists at Chris McMillan do amazing cuts and styles and editorial styling for magazine shoots and I wanted more than anything to be able to do the same, but again, I had to wait. And picture me standing at my salon chair before I started booking up, just waiting—and waiting and waiting—for my schedule to fill up. This was before we had iPhones to distract us! That one was a special kind of mind fuck, because when you're in a small salon, everyone can see who's busy and whose chair is empty. Nobody wants to be noticed for their empty chair.

For as long as I've been working, every time I think I have things figured out, I've had to slow my roll and have the patience and humility to learn something new. After I'd mastered one haircut, I would realize that I needed to learn a different one, and then it was another hair texture, and then there was editorial hair, and next was learning how to do runway hair. Maybe this doesn't sound that hard to you, but believe it or not, there are a lot of technical aspects of doing hair that take time and patience to learn. If a client is walking the red carpet, I have to make sure her hair will look good at any angle throughout the night, even if there's bad weather. For an editorial shoot, I have to know what side the photographer is shooting from, and what the lighting will look like, and how the style fits with the makeup and the backdrop. For TV appearances, I have to know which side of the face the camera will get, and when my client is performing onstage or walking a runway, I have to make sure the style can withstand lots of movement, quick changes, and sweat—and, oh, you have twenty minutes to get it right. There is always another thing you have to learn, and if you're impatient and try to do a look you're not ready for, there's a very good chance it won't end well.

I've found that patience comes more easily with age, but if you're feeling that extra-special angst of wanting everything, like, now, take some deep breaths and remember what you already know deep down. There is no rush. Your time will come.

HUSTLE PORN ISN'T THE WHOLE STORY

Hustle porn, as you probably know, is twenty-first-century vernacular for all that social media content that makes working 24/7 and never taking a break and running from one meeting or job to the next look exciting and sexy. I get that it's cool to see the behind-the-scenes of building a business, and I'm all for the transparency of showing how many people and meetings and late nights go into building a product; but glamorizing the hustle is just dishonest. Sometimes hustling feels like, well, a hustle. In other words, it's not especially fun. Our current culture has assigned a lot of value and status to busyness, as if the more jam-packed your schedule, the more important you are. And I'm sorry, but that's effed up. It's unhealthy. Overloading your schedule and overcommitting and trying to fit twenty-five hours into a day can cause actual stress and illness, not to mention the fact that it prevents you from having any time to enjoy the so-called success it brings. Burnout is a very real possibility when you have a job, a side hustle, and a side hustle to your side hustle. ("You have as many hours in a day as Beyoncé" is supposed to be inspirational, but all it really does is shame you for taking a breather and *not* doing seventy-five jobs at once.) If you find yourself dreading even the smallest task, or feeling overwhelmed the moment you have to add anything to your to-do list, you might be suffering from burnout without even realizing it. And that's not only unhealthy, it's dangerous—burnout can lead to depression or exhaustion. I'm not trying to scare you, but I *am* hoping that this might serve as a wake-up call. Because when that kind of nonstop grind becomes the standard, it's bad for everyone.

Here's the thing that a lot of people don't realize: in some regards, a *true* measure of success is when you start to get a little less busy. I hustled for years and years, but one of the first times I really felt like I'd made it was when I was able to hire a team around me to take on some of my workload. Being able to off-load and delegate rather than having to do everything myself—that was one of the biggest measures of success.

I'll fully own that in the past I've been guilty of posting my own "hustle," not only to inspire people but also to prove to myself or to my peers that I'm busting my ass as hard as the next guy, as if it's a competition. It's a lot of "Stay tuned! Working on this! Can't wait to share what I'm doing!" and it can feel like the underlying context is actually: *Who sacrificed and suffered the most today in service of their work? Who is seeing their family the least or hasn't exercised in a month?* That is a competition I no longer want to win, and I don't encourage anyone else to engage in it, either.

I'm constantly telling people that they don't need to put pressure on themselves to do all the things, but I say it as someone who has put *a ton* of pressure on herself to do all the things FOR YEARS. But with age I've seen that a lot of my self-imposed suffering was unnecessary. Yes, I needed to put in the work and dedicate the time and suffer the pinpricks and bleached fingers, but there's a difference between working hard and burning out, and I've been guilty of slipping over onto the wrong side of that line. I'm not proud of it. Again, I didn't have a blueprint for the career I wanted, so I had to learn and make mistakes as I went. Looking back today, I can see those mistakes clearly.

The good news is that I'm finally at a place where my priorities have shifted and I want to work to live, not live to work. Because work is satisfying and fulfilling and even inspiring, but it's not *every*thing. The moment the thing you're passionate about takes over your life in such a way that rather than wanting to do it you feel like you *need* to do it, you start veering into unhealthy territory. I worry that, amid the posts and tweets and hustle porn where everyone is "killing it!" and "go go go" and "creating something BIG," we forget to acknowledge that the work it takes to find success can be exhausting and requires a lot of sacrifice— and can be a recipe for a pretty miserable life. Instead of glorifying the hustle, I wish we'd talk about it for what it is and acknowledge the fact that, as a culture, especially in America, we have a messed-up view of "the Business of Busyness." Being a workaholic should not be an aspiration, even though a lot of people I know identify with that label and take some kind of pride in it. Take it from someone who had to learn the hard way: being so consumed by work that you become sick with stress, give up on exercise, and never see the people you love should not be an aspiration and is not sustainable. Running on empty is not #selfcare.

READY, SET, CREATE

If you've read this whole chapter and you find yourself thinking, *Fine, Jen, I get it, my ascent to success is going to take a while, but can you please give me some actual advice about how I can get started NOW???* . . . then, okay, you deserve an assignment. You may have a long, hard road ahead of you, but the good news is that one thing you can do today for sure is start making content. No matter what type of entrepreneur you are, every business needs marketing visuals (thanks, internet), and today they have to be better than ever to get a consumer's attention. Understanding how to make quality content is critical to succeeding in just about any small business. Want to sell houses? You need great content. Want to sell granola? You need great content. Want to sell yourself as a makeup artist or hairstylist or designer? You need great content (and great lighting).

So how do you make great content? Practice. Find someone whose dream is to be a photographer and someone else who wants to be a stylist (of people or food or houses), and start playing around with ideas that will benefit all of your businesses or portfolios. Get creative, make inspo boards, think about color palettes, and create visuals that will make someone stop and look. That's it! That's your first assignment. In any product- or service-based business, you need good photos and a willingness to promote yourself in order to compete with everyone else out there. But remember, creating content that gets noticed takes time. I used to spend hours on Tumblr and the IG Explore page to get my creativity flowing, but I've since stopped trying to get to the end of my Insta feed, because my limited free time is better spent creating quality content and interacting directly with my followers than watching what everyone else is doing. And if you don't see anyone in TV, movies, or magazines that looks like you or relates to you? Even more reason to go out there and create it and be seen and heard.

So be proactive. And get creative. And have the persistence to do it again tomorrow and the next day and the day after that. It's going to be a hustle—one filled with excitement and exhaustion and determination and obstacles—but that's cool. You've got TIME.

St. George—me and my new Saturn whip ready to go take
on the big city of LA—1999

Bella Hadid for CFDA awards—2017

Hailey Bieber on her wedding day—2019

Ambushing Kendall Jenner in a photo booth—2018

CHAPTER FOUR
IT'S NOT ABOUT YOU. NO, REALLY, IT'S NOT ABOUT YOU.

did the math recently, and it turns out that after working in a salon for more than a decade, with ten to fifteen women in my chair every day, I have talked for an hour or so at a time with nearly 10,000 people for more than 26,000 hours. Where's my psychology degree, people?? That's a hell of a lot of time discussing other people's feelings, fears, hopes, and dreams, not to mention what they're doing on Saturday night or how they're handling their recent breakup. I swear, I feel like a therapist, and the cardinal rule of being a successful therapist? It's not about you. Well, okay, maybe it's also about swearing to protect your clients' privacy, but we already covered not being a blabbermouth in Chapter Two.

It's pretty easy for me to give a client my full attention—it comes kind of naturally to me. Maybe that's because I was taught from an early age to pay attention to the people around me. Bettering your community while bettering yourself is pretty central to the whole Mormon upbringing, and it's basically a reflex for me to invest my attention in other people. When I started working in hair salons, I realized that the most in-demand stylists took the same approach to their work—in this case, focusing more on their client community than themselves—and it made an obvious difference in terms of their success. When my career expanded into content creation and then into building OUAI, I was quick to notice that the same principle held true: those who could really hone in on the needs of their readers or their followers or consumers were the ones who were killing it in their fields.

In my time at Estilo, I had ample opportunity to observe the hairstylists on the floor and see what worked for them and what didn't. There were plenty of stylists driven by greed and ego—always chasing higher-profile clients and trying to demand a higher price for their time—but they weren't the people who booked out months ahead. The common denominator for the stylists with packed schedules was that they were totally focused on the needs of their clients. Of course they were also talented stylists, but when you work at a top salon in Beverly Hills, all the stylists are talented. The most successful stylists were excited to see each and every client (or at least they were great actors) and asked a lot of questions throughout the appointment. Besides being good at doing hair, they were good at listening, and that combination is what brought clients back time after time and kept them paying for expensive cuts. Celebrities come into Beverly Hills salons pretty regularly, and I always noticed the few stylists who treated the "regular-person" client as well as they treated the A-lister. I remember watching Robert Ramos, Reny Salamon, and Philip Carreon, whose clients included Jessica Alba, Winona Ryder, Bette Midler, and Stevie Nicks, and they were so sincere and kind to everyone. They invested their attention in each and every client and developed genuine connections with them. You could look at that and say, "Wow, they're so humble to still pay attention to the little people, even with all of those celebrity clients," but I think it's kind of the opposite. Without that attitude of service and sustained investment of attention, they wouldn't *have* those celebrity clients. As you begin to grow and take on more high-profile projects and assignments in your career, it's important not to cut corners or stop doing the very things that landed you those opportunities. In other words: a little ego can be a dangerous thing.

Over the past twenty years or so, I've seen this lesson play out over and over, across all lines of work. Make it about you, and your moment in the spotlight will pass in a heartbeat. Focus on others, and those people will keep coming back, and you'll keep working. Today, this lesson is the first one I impart to the young women I hire. If they want to succeed, they have to remember that the job is about the client—making them feel good and safe and comfortable. We are in a SERVICE industry, after all. If you're waiting for a more exciting person to sit down in the chair, or you're posting to your Insta stories instead of giving the client your full attention? Or you're making your client sit and wait for you while you finish a phone call? Then you're not doing your job, because your job is to take care of the person in front of you—the whole person—no matter who they are. Your job is to make your clients feel cared for and special.

Part of focusing your attention on the client is tuning into what they want from you. In any business, you need to sort of be a chameleon. Maybe you have a client or a colleague or a boss who's super-high-energy, and even though you're typically a little more laid-back, you know that if you want to connect with them and make them happy, you need to do a shot of espresso and a few power poses before a meeting. Or maybe it's the opposite—you take it down a notch to connect with a client who's soft-spoken, because you don't want to talk over them or miss something important. Whether you're a doctor or a teacher or a lawyer or a secretary or an entrepreneur, the people who are the most successful at their jobs are the ones who can mold their approach around the needs of other people, who can put their own ego aside to allow another person to feel seen and heard. I constantly tell my assistants that they need to take the temperature in the room. Adjust to the energy your client is putting out there. Don't come bounding in trying to set the tone. Some clients want to chat or confide; they want a sympathetic ear. Others just want to put in some earbuds and close their eyes for an hour. It's our job to adjust to them, to give them the best possible experience. In other words, follow, don't lead. It's not about you.

Now, to be clear, I'm not saying that anyone—no matter what your line of work—should check their personality at the door. Not at all. Your personality is as important to your success as your talent, and honestly it might be more like

70 percent personality and 30 percent talent. Especially these days, when there's so much success to be gained from social content, which only resonates when you're being authentic. When I started out, personalities were not on display the way they are now. On one hand, that was great, because you could just put your head down and do the work and not have to worry about this entirely separate aspect of business-building—though even then your clients weren't going to return if you were a total wet blanket or an intense angry creative. Personality is essential, but you have to toe the line. You can be friendly and pleasant and outgoing and fun while still being respectful and remembering that the work you're doing is about making someone else's life better. Because you can't empower others to be their best selves if you're not listening to their needs, and you can't help make anyone's life better if the person you're really trying to serve is yourself.

ASK QUESTIONS, LEARN FROM EVERYONE

We live in a filtered world where everyone looks shiny and happy and confident at all times, so it can be scary to admit that you don't have it all together. Remember, you see everyone's successes and not their struggles. So many people on social are living that fake-it-till-you-make-it life, and that's not necessarily a bad thing, but if you're pretending like you have all the answers, you're cutting yourself off from a lot of opportunities to ask questions. You're cutting yourself off from growth. When you embrace an it's-not-about-me mindset, you realize pretty quickly that the people around you have a lot of information that you don't, and they have a lot to offer that can benefit you in the long run. Getting comfortable asking questions is probably the best thing you can do for your career and, frankly, for your life.

When I started working at The Chris McMillan Salon, a lot of the staff there were scared to look Chris in the eye. That's how big a deal he was. But I was intrigued by him and in awe of him, and I didn't pretend otherwise. (I'm still in awe of him, because he's an incredible artist and an incredible personality. I can hear his laugh as I type this— it's beautiful and infectious.) I wanted to be around Chris, and even more, I wanted to know *what he was doing* that made clients flock to him, so that I could do it, too.

I've always been a curious person, and I wanted to learn from Chris on both a personal and a professional level. I knew from day one that every moment in his salon was an opportunity to be a sponge, and I couldn't blow that. So I became the tagalong he couldn't quite shake. I was like that annoying sidekick girl in *West Side Story*—God, she had cute hair. Luckily, because it was clear I was coming from an authentic place of wanting to learn, he didn't seem to mind me hanging around. I took this same curious approach with every stylist who would tolerate me. Luckily, a lot of very talented and gracious mentors tolerated me for a long time.

Have you ever had a question you were too nervous to ask—for fear of sounding dumb, or because you figured that someone else had already asked the same thing? Have you ever wished you'd had the courage to raise your hand

and question the status quo? Asking "why" is really powerful. It can change the trajectory of careers, or relationships,
or even your health. Maybe you fear you're overstepping
or digging into areas that aren't your business. Maybe you
think you're too old to be asking certain questions. Forget
that. When people see that you want to learn from them,
they'll embrace your curiosity. Once you check your ego,
you'll open yourself up to so much support from other people. You have nothing to lose by asking dumb questions.*

Finding my place in the hairstyling community was especially meaningful for me because I grew up feeling like
I never really fit in. I was good at being friends with the
jocks and the nerds and the drama geeks in high school—I
was always cool with everyone, and generally stayed under
the radar—but I never really felt like I truly connected
with anyone besides my best friend, Lindsay. (That could
have been due to the fact that I didn't look or act like everyone around me in a sea of white Mormon goody-two-shoe
kids.) Once I got into the big city and the salon environment, it was like I'd found my people.† Back in the pre-
internet days, if you didn't have a client in your chair, you
passed the time by hanging out in the back of the salon,
talking with your peers. When I was socializing with the
other stylists, I wasn't just learning about the business. I
was learning about the people—who they were and how
they lived and how they thought about things. It was exciting for me to be among a mix of cultures and religions

---

* *That was a trick. There are no dumb questions.*

† *As it turned out, "my people" were mostly gay men, and they were
hard to find in Utah.*

and backgrounds. It was fun, but it was also an important learning experience, because if you want to be successful in any business—especially in today's increasingly fractured society—you need to be able to connect with all kinds of people. And I mean genuinely connect with people. Like, put-your-phone-down-and-make-eye-contact-and-learn-from-people kind of connection.

As my career gained momentum, I never stopped wanting to learn. The more people I met and the more experiences I had, the more knowledge I could soak in. In the early days, I often did small editorial jobs for ZERO money so I could learn what editors were looking for and get schooled in on-set etiquette. I would sneak backstage at fashion shows (this is when attendance was monitored on paper lists and not iPads) and set up my kit to assist wherever I could, again for no money, because it was like going to hair university. I didn't care how I was going to make ends meet, because this was how I was going to master a skill set. I learned from the best of the best and made connections that I treasure to this day, the most notable being Guido Palau, a true legend in the hair world. Somehow, I got onto his assistant list. Guido can perfectly execute one intricate look on set, and he can just as easily create a hundred different looks for major designers of fashion houses all over the world. This guy is like the Elvis of hair, and watching how he stayed laser-focused and perfectly poised backstage, even with pure chaos unraveling all around him, was an invaluable lesson for me. I've never seen someone create the way Guido does.

I started out in hair knowing NOTHING at all, and so many talented human beings shared what they knew and helped me develop my own approach and aesthetic. The only thing I *did* know back then was to listen to the people who were wiser than me, and thank God I did.

IN SERVICE OF CELEBRITY

How do you work with celebrities? This is something people ask me All. The. Time. And, yes, it takes hard work and, yes, it takes talent and, absolutely, yes, it takes a decent amount of luck, but perhaps above all, working in service of celebrity talent is about being humble—because those situations are most certainly not about you. First of all, you have to be very, very, *very* comfortable with the idea that you're not going to be the prettiest person in the room. You will never be the center of attention, nor should you want to be (if you do, working with celebrities is not for you). There is a hierarchy on set, and—spoiler alert!— hair and makeup isn't at the top of the totem pole. To do the kind of work that I do, you have to be okay with being the help, climbing into the back seat, and having paps yell at you to move out of the way. In other jobs there's probably fewer paparazzi, but if you find yourself in service of any- one high-profile in your field, you'll have to take the back seat (more figuratively this time, but still) and let them be in the spotlight, even if it feels like you're the one getting your hands dirty and doing the grueling work. That's just the hard truth of being a working adult.

Another thing? You have to learn how to manage your own fangirl reaction. Working with a famous person is not about the OMG factor for you, it's about skillfully and professionally providing a service for the person who has hired you. This sounds obvious, I know, but when you're standing there next to an actor or model or performer you've admired your whole life, it's a real pinch-me moment. As a service provider, you need to keep in mind that celebrities spend their lives in the zoo-like limelight where people stare at them all the time, so it's important to create a safe space where they can trust the professionals around them. This is a tough one, because it can be challenging to walk into a room with the likes of Kendall Jenner, Hailey Bieber, or Bella Hadid and not gawk—I mean, these women are truly gorgeous, and it can be kind of breathtaking. But ogling the client is not respectful, and not even the most famous faces in the world want to be gawked at behind the scenes.

This is a skill I've had to work on over the years. I'll never forget the first time I got called to work with Gwen Stefani. When I hung up, I let out a shriek that probably made dogs howl. I was OBSESSED with No Doubt as a teenager . . . her posters used to cover my walls and now I was going to be responsible for Gwen's iconic hair?? In moments like that, it can feel impossible to avoid freaking out and turning into a rambling fangirl. But I've seen other people do that, and let me tell you, it's not cute. When a magazine editor gets red in the face upon meeting the celebrity she's supposed to interview, or a photographer is short of breath because their childhood crush is standing before them, or a makeup artist has shaky hands when she's about to work on her bucket-list A-lister, it's awkward for everyone. Telling someone how much they mean to you is great, but there's a time and a place for that. Do all the shrieking you want in the privacy of your own home, but when you're with the client, pull yourself together. And don't fall into the chatty trap. It's a human tendency to talk about ourselves when we get nervous, which kind of goes against the whole it's-not-about-you thing. It's also common to just talk nonstop, period, when nerves hit. Take a deep breath, read the room, and do your best work so you get hired back again.

In short: if you choose to work with famous people, you need to embrace the fact that you are not the star, and you need to be comfortable enough with yourself for that not to be a struggle. But the good news is that celebrities have really great food on their riders, and you'll usually get all the free snacks you want on set.

SOLVING OTHER PEOPLE'S PROBLEMS

When I decided to launch OUAI, I was driven by the knowledge that building a thriving business stems from creating something that solves other people's problems. When most people think of successful businesses, they probably think in terms of cash and revenue and profit. But for me, the goal of creating a product line was to fulfill a need, create something I didn't see on the market, and improve other people's lives. Don't get me wrong—financial success is a critical, and enjoyable, part of running a business, too. But the kind of success most entrepreneurs dream of doesn't happen if they aren't serving their clients or customers, first and foremost. When it comes to OUAI, whether we're brainstorming a new product or crafting the messages for packaging, I begin by asking our communities what they want and need—a product that saves them time? Or smells different? Or doesn't smell at all? (Often we ask our followers directly and work with our own curated focus groups—thank you, sweet baby Jesus, for technology.) Frankly, all good businesses know they need to focus on the consumer first. Sure, there are people who only think about themselves and their bottom line, but that's not the kind of business I'm interested in leading. I wholeheartedly believe that clients or consumers or coworkers can sense when your heart isn't in it or if you're not being transparent. Karma doesn't come back to serve you when you're phoning it in or being dishonest. If you need proof of this, watch the Fyre Festival documentary.

What I've learned over the years is that all anyone wants is help being their best. Everyone wants to flourish. I've known this instinctively for a long time, even if I couldn't always articulate it. I started making collages on my Instagram long before that was trendy. I wanted to inspire creativity, but in an accessible way, and those posts did really well. I quickly realized that if I built my page as a place where people could get helpful information that they could use on their own, they would come back. And that's so much more interesting to me than constantly promoting my own work, though as I've mentioned, this type of teaching was pretty rare for a long time in my industry. When I started out, hairstyling was super-competitive. You didn't share what you knew. Stylists certainly would never teach a class. On an individual level, they were solving their clients' problems by giving them great hair, but they weren't offering solutions for people who couldn't afford $200, $300, even $600 haircuts—it just wasn't done. But I love to connect the dots. To connect people. I like helping and I like learning, so as soon as I had the platform, I flipped the switch and let more people in on what I knew. I wanted to share information not just to help people look great for a big event but to help other professionals in my community.

I'm going to let you in on a secret, though I hope you'll keep reading even after my big reveal: my desire to empower other people is the reason I've been successful, and that same vision can drive your success, too. I launched Mane Addicts because I realized there was a gaping hole in the hair community. There was no digital destination for people who were interested in hair to find cutting-edge industry information or get to know the talented artists behind the looks, or for the people who lived far from Hollywood red carpets or trendy New York City salons to learn how they could get their own celeb-style hair at home. And there wasn't a good destination for up-and-coming stylists to learn from seasoned professionals, which is why I started Mane University. Early on, I saw the internet as a tool to bring hair-challenged consumers and professional stylists and brands together. I wanted to build a global hair community and continue to showcase diverse cultures and talent while we grew as a platform.

OUAI started in the same, well, way. Before we came on the scene, every piece of hair-product messaging out there showcased a woman who clearly had a professional blowout, or a model wearing a wig on set with the wind blowing through her shiny, healthy, fake hair. But that's not realistic. People are busy. They want to do their hair quickly, look good, and get out the door. I know this firsthand, because I'm a busy woman and my friends and followers are busy women. I tried to create a product that gave those same amazing-hair-day results but also fit into real women's real lives, using the hair they were born with. I wanted to give people the tools to become the best version of themselves so that they could focus on conquering the world rather than fixating on their appearance. By concentrating on community and connections and empowering others instead of zeroing in on getting ahead . . . well, I got ahead. So if you have a dream, or an idea, take a moment to look at it from this perspective—what hole are you filling? What already exists in the space? What does it look like globally? What can you offer that others aren't? That understanding will help propel you forward.

The idea of being of service is pretty key to success in social media, too. As anyone who follows me knows, I feature other people's products and other people's work when I think it will help my followers, and you'd probably be surprised at how often I've been advised to stop doing that. Agents or managers have warned me that shining the spotlight away from myself and my business is too risky. Why build a platform to showcase another hairstylist's work when I can sell my own? Why talk up anyone else's fragrance if OUAI has killer perfume too? But I respect the needs of my followers. I want them to trust me and to know that I'll show them whatever I think will be helpful, rather than selling them on things that line my pockets. (FWIW, I don't get paid when I share other people's work.) I believe in promoting yourself, for sure, but if your business is only focused on self-promotion, your clients or followers will get bored quickly. Also, you're just lying. I would be straight-up lying if I didn't show my beauty closet lined with products I'm gifted or I buy myself. I've muted more than a few people on Instagram because I got sick of seeing that kind of self-serving tunnel vision. What everyone craves these days is authenticity, and luckily, that's free and easily accessible to all of us (or at least, most of us). The more you pay attention to other people or accounts or companies, and the more you share information that your followers will actually care about, the faster your own platform, and your opportunities, will grow.

LEADING THE ~~OUAI~~ WAY

When it comes to business, solving other people's problems is about more than clients and consumers. Any good boss knows that leadership involves setting aside your own ego and listening to and investing in your employees. I learned that lesson pretty quickly after launching OUAI.

We were a start-up, which meant we had a skeleton crew tasked with doing a *lot* of work. The beginning stages of a business are stressful for the founder and investors but even more so for the employees doing the day-to-day tasks. There were so many demands on us—we had to build out our marketing campaigns, figure out which products we wanted to launch with, sell to retail and e-commerce stores, send out PR packages, brainstorm our follow-up products—and the nervous energy of the entire team was palpable. I'd walk through our small office and hear nothing but the *clack-clack-clack* of fingers on a keyboard. Everyone was on overdrive trying to fit in one more thing before the day's end.

It was a real challenge for me to figure out how to step up and be the kind of leader my employees needed and deserved, but what I learned pretty quickly was that no matter what worries or stress I felt as the founder, I couldn't project those issues onto my team. Part of my job as a boss was to be a shield, and protect everyone who worked for me from unnecessary pressure. I wanted to create a friendly vibe while still keeping things professional, and I wanted everyone to always feel heard.

I learned quickly that when you're a leader at work, your mood will set the tone for everyone else. If I come into the office feeling pissy and snap at everyone who makes a mistake, that's going to create a hostile environment, where everyone is on edge and scared to offer up their ideas. If I approach my team with an "everybody has a voice, good ideas can come from anywhere" vibe, and I'm smiling and laughing and being respectful no matter where someone falls on the org chart, everyone else will follow suit.

Even in my hairstyling work, which is obviously not in an office, it's important to me that my assistants know I understand and respect that they have a life outside the job. I don't want to suffocate them. I expect a lot from myself and the people I employ, so I try to reward good behavior and give them freedom when the work is done. In fact, freedom is one of the best incentives I have to keep top-performing employees happy and engaged. I try to give them both the support and the autonomy necessary to do their jobs, but I don't micromanage. I believe that allowing good people to do their work without breathing down their necks is one of the best ways you can show trust and respect. And the more an employee feels that trust, the better they will perform for you.

I didn't figure this all out by myself. In 2018, after OUAI

established itself as a company to watch in the hair-care space, we decided it was time to hire a CEO. The prospect made me nervous, because I'd heard so many stories of outside leadership coming in to fledgling companies and destroying the culture. I was a protective mama bear when it came to OUAI, because one of our wonderful and rare attributes was that we had an unfiltered, authentic voice. I didn't want to lose that.

I ended up going on a lot of bad "dates" with stiff, buttoned-up men before we found and hired Colin Walsh, our current CEO. By the time he joined the team, I had figured out how I liked to lead when things were going well, but steering the ship during harder periods was another matter entirely. Colin taught me that during challenging times, it's crucial for leaders to be positive and encouraging, because anything less can cause people to panic and make decisions from a place of defensiveness or fear rather than possibility. When the stakes are high, the worst thing a leader can do is fan the flames of anxiety and put more pressure on the team as they try to make something happen. Remember: it's not about you. Translation: If you're panicked, suck it up, at least until you get home. That doesn't mean lying to your colleagues or being less than transparent, but it does mean being poised even in times of uncertainty.

In the years since launching OUAI, I've discovered that I have a strength for inspiring creatives to do their best work and take risks. That has been incredibly rewarding. At both OUAI and Mane Addicts, a wave of pride washes over me when I walk into the office and see the ambitious talent, the creativity, and the commitment of the teams we've built. Proud mama bear, remember?

DON'T BUY INTO YOUR OWN HYPE

I have been incredibly lucky within my profession, because after decades of serving celebrities, I have become relatively well known myself. I call it being celeb-adjacent-ish. Not a celebrity, for sure, but I have recognition now that I certainly did not in the first, say, fifteen years of my career. As your own profile grows, it's even more important to remind yourself that it's always about the client, because even when the success comes and you're the one calling the shots, you still need to keep your ego in check. You may see me in an Instagram story chatting with a famous client, but when that camera is off I am digging in and doing my job, stressing until they walk out the door, just like I did ten years ago. In the world of everyone wanting to make a name for themselves, it's a practice every day to stay humble and not be affected by any additional attention. But it's an essential practice, if you want to keep working. I know I sound like I'm lecturing, but I have seen what happens when ego takes over and suddenly artists start to act like they're more important than the talent. Remember, at the end of the day, it's the talent who does the hiring. If you treat your clients like an afterthought, they'll happily write those checks to someone else.

There are a lot of different ways people can earn praise or attention in their careers, and obviously it varies depending on the industry. Maybe public recognition for you means being invited to a special conference or summit; being name-checked in an industry newsletter or magazine; or being asked to deliver the keynote speech at a conference of your peers. In the styling world, some of that attention comes from awards. But putting stock in that kind of manufactured competition can be dangerous. If I'm up for an award against a group of stylists, I politely decline my invitation to the ceremony. I don't even post about it. I hate the idea of being "better" than anyone else, and I think awards are a dangerous and subjective "honor." I understand that recognition is gratifying, and the times when I've been awarded something independently—because of my own work and not because I'm doing it "better" than someone else—I have been honored to accept. But I've never thought I was the most talented hairstylist out there, and I don't like winning something at the expense of someone else. People going home feeling like losers? Lame. (It's also important to note that everything is a business, and awards shows are paid by advertisers. I find that the accolades lose their sentiment once you realize that.) My perception of myself and the goals that I set for myself are personal. If I were in this industry for the accolades or the attention, I probably would have burned out a decade ago.

This isn't to say that I don't care about career achievements. There are plenty of wins that feel great; they just don't come at the expense of anyone else. I feel accomplished when a product launch goes well. When my team is laughing in our meetings and having fun at work. When I send my assistants to do a client's hair and they do an incredible job. When I've worked with John Galliano at Dior shows or when I did my first *Vogue* cover with Gwen Stefani or when I worked with Annie Leibovitz—those were milestones that made me feel like I'd arrived. But I'm also highly aware that no matter how popular you get, moments in the spotlight are fleeting. The minute you start believing your own hype is the minute you stop being good at your job.

FAKING IT

Because the world is a cold and confusing place, I'll be honest with you that while I generally don't endorse pretending to know things you don't, and I nearly always choose to ask questions, sometimes—for the sake of the client!—you do have to fake it. You hairstylists out there, listen close. Clients are like babies and dogs: they can smell fear. If you start shaking the minute you pick up the scissors, you don't get a second chance. In my years on the floor, I saw everything, including a new stylist accidentally cut a client's ear. The stylist was talking with his hands, and unfortunately the ear was the victim. One time I grabbed what I thought were my thinning shears, to take weight off a client's hair, but I actually grabbed my regular scissors. I started cutting and took out a chunk of hair before I realized my mistake. Then I pretended nothing happened and fixed it without skipping a beat (and prayed there were no witnesses). Another time I was styling a celebrity and he was so beautiful that I simply could not concentrate (I know, I know, I wasn't following my own "no fangirling" rule).* He wanted me to bleach a small part of his hair, and I swear I was so distracted by his perfect features that I forgot to put in the peroxide, so I ended up with a mixture

---

* *I should probably add that he was a heartthrob in the '90s, which was peak heartthrob-obsession time for me.*

of just powder and water. In other words—I put some stuff in his hair but it didn't change the color at all. I took off the foils and said, "This looks amazing!" Because what else could I do? "It does, thanks!" he replied.

Phew.

I'm happy to say I haven't had too many serious "oh fuck" moments over the years, but when you do, you've got to roll with the punches, because the people around you react to your reactions. Sometimes you can listen carefully and do everything a client asks, and it turns out they didn't want what they thought they wanted. Or they didn't accurately describe what they wanted, and now they're not happy. Maybe you can relate—maybe you've worked hard on a project, and you took direction from the client and tried to deliver what they were looking for . . . but something was lost in translation, and now they're pissed. I always try to remember that my clients take their cues from me. If you react questionably, it's going to set off red flags. Sometimes just hearing them out and making a few tweaks will address their concerns. Don't let your ego take a situation from bad to worse. Be open to receiving feedback, and make it work.

Because while the job's not about you, when things don't go well, someone will always want to make it about you.

In Dallas, Texas, exploring a potential lab for OUAI—2014

CHAPTER FIVE
FINDING
MY OUAI

I n 2014, after years of styling women of all different eth-
nicities and hair types, two friends and I—one of whom
was Jewish with curly hair and the other Black with
textured hair—had the idea to open a blow-dry bar that
would cater to a wider range of hair textures and styles
than those dominating the market. We wanted it to be
a luxe experience while being more inclusive, with stylists who could master a wide variety of looks. As part of
our business planning, we dug into the market research:
What products were out there that served different hair
types? What would we need to carry in the salons? What
would our stylists use? Over the years, I had become used
to brands sending me samples directly, but now I was
walking the aisles of stores like Sephora and Ulta to see
who carried what, and I was looking online to see which
companies stood out in the digital space. I was also curious
about social presence—I knew there were only a few hair
brands that were making the most of what Insta and other
platforms had to offer.

I still think that our blow-dry bar was a good idea, but in

the end the three of us just didn't have time for it. I had my clients and Mane Addicts, and my would-be business partners were a high-profile publicist and a high-profile event planner, both of whom were swamped with their day jobs. None of us had the bandwidth to support the needs for the business on a full-time basis, so the idea fizzled (not before I invested my own money, but we learn from our mistakes, right?). Still, everything I had learned during the market research phase stuck with me. After months of trying products and smelling them and inspecting packaging and reading ingredients, what I learned was that none of it spoke to me or my friends. The marketing copy all felt very commercial—rather than calling something what it was, each product had, like, seventeen descriptive names ("try our powder puff volumizing talcum texture dry shampoo spray!")—and the packaging felt very bland and corporate. The advertisements—which almost always featured white women with thick, flowing hair—were completely unrelatable (seriously, look at any hair ad pre-2015), and the scents were either bubblegum or smelled like a bad vintage perfume. Nothing modern or musky or floral. And crazily enough, a lot of brands were still animal-testing and using sulfates. At that point, I knew from connecting with my followers that millennials cared about their overall health and the health of the environment. They didn't want products with toxins, and they definitely wanted to support companies whose product-testing was cruelty–free. They were also starting to pay attention to the people behind the brands.

While I'd been collecting all this research, I was still

working as a hairstylist, sending my clients to the health food store to get biotin or fish oil because very few beauty brands were selling hair supplements. Next I would send them to the department store for dry shampoo or gel or mousse. We needed twenty different products to put together one look. It became glaringly obvious that there was a space in the hair industry that needed to be filled—where were the multipurpose, nontoxic, easy-to-use products for real women? Eventually I couldn't ignore the nudge that told me I should be the one to fill it.

PARDON THE DISRUPTION

By the time I sat down to put together a one-sheeter— basically a brand guide and mission statement—I understood two opposing truths about the beauty industry: it was changing, but it was also stagnant. Social media was revolutionizing the way people found products, but the big businesses were slow to evolve, and executives at major companies didn't understand the wild world of new media. Brands that had been around for decades were stuck in their traditional ways, more inclined to play it safe than to invest money into adapting to the younger, social-savvy consumer. Any time I'd been pitched collaborations with hair-care brands in the past, I'd politely declined—I was underwhelmed and even discouraged by the proposals. The big companies seemed out of touch, unaware that the best place to find their consumers would be on Instagram or YouTube or Snapchat. After all, most of them were run by old white men in boardrooms who didn't really have a clue about how young women take care of their hair. The recipe was always to tell your consumer what they need rather than ask. I had worked with enough legacy brands at that point to know it would take a long time for them to change. I knew I understood something they didn't, and I was ready to disrupt.

Despite having what I knew was a great idea, I faced one pretty major challenge: I wasn't a businessperson. I didn't know how to create a business plan or attract investors. But I did know that you don't always need to know what you're doing. Sometimes you have to figure it out along the way, and I'd already done that plenty. I'd figured out how to get my own place and make my own money when I got to L.A., and then how to get my beauty license and become a confident hairdresser when I started working in salons. By 2014, I was in "why not me?" mode. The days of "how did I get here, who do I think I am?" were gone, and now it was "I'm a human being and all the entrepreneurs and disruptors are human beings, so why not me?"

I sat down at my computer and started putting ideas on a page. I wrote down three questions: *What do we do? Who are we doing it for? What is the benefit?* Then I tried to articulate the answers: we create simple, effective, and cleanly packaged hair products for busy women who want to get ready quickly without sacrificing style, and who want to feel confident enough in their look that they're happy to be tagged in photos. I made a spreadsheet with tabs for categories like "scent" and "labs and formulation" and "supplements" and "packaging and distribution," writing down the names of relevant companies that came up repeatedly in my research or in conversations with other beauty entrepreneurs. I sent a lot of unreturned emails, made lots of unreturned phone calls. I may not have known what I was doing, but I also knew I had nothing to lose.

GETTING DOWN TO BUSINESS

Going from killer idea to killer PowerPoint is not easy. There are entire books devoted to the topic, and if you're trying to start your own business you should absolutely go read a couple of them.* One thing I learned quickly: if I had any hope of getting a business off the ground, the first thing I needed was funding. I sent a lot of "If you know anybody looking to invest in a budding business, let me know" emails . . . and I got a lot of "You're not famous enough yet" or "I would wait ten years" in return. But sometimes it only takes one believer, and mine came in the form of one of my clients in a Dubai salon, who was a friend of Lorraine Schwartz's, one of my mentors. This client had her own skin-care line and understood what I was trying to do and offered to put up the money to help me get off the ground.

Once I had a financial partner, we decided to hire someone to do an analysis of the hair-care industry and describe how our products would stand out from the pack. Tony Yumul, a friend and fellow former Mormon from Utah (whose

---

* *Business books I especially like are* What You Really Need to Lead, *by Robert Steven Kaplan;* Unfinished Business, *by Anne-Marie Slaughter; and* Tell to Win, *by Peter Guber.*

couch I crashed on when I first moved to L.A.), had started his own creative design agency, and he told me the first thing I needed to do was articulate my "founder's story." The gist of that story was simple. I wanted to launch a brand that was socially driven—that meant creating products largely dictated by online focus groups and crowdsourcing and user polls. I wanted to offer a line of multi-use products (no more ten-step regimens for one look) that made #hairgoals a reality, without a glam squad. And I wanted to design packaging that women were proud to keep out on their counter or feature in photos, with a website that had easy-to-follow instructions for a variety of looks.

Before I could launch anything, though, I needed a name. I was inspired by the time I'd spent working at fashion shows in Paris and by the women there whose street style was effortlessly cool. I created an inspo board and pinned images of models and Chanel's minimal packaging from the 1920s. Tony and I went through a ton of different French words and their meanings. For a brief moment we were going to call it *Jeté*, but I liked that the word *ouais* was a casual way of saying *yes* in French ("ouais" is a kind of equivalent of "yeah," but somehow *waaaay* more chic). It also sort of looked Hawaiian, once we dropped the *s*, with all its vowels in a row. And being the cornball that I am, I also loved that it could easily be used to create puns. Oh, and it had to be written in all caps. OUAI it was.

Once I had funding and a name, it was time to actually create a product. My investor and I traveled a lot and scheduled a ton of meetings—we toured hair-care laboratories, met with fragrance houses and aerosol labs and supplement labs, connected with packaging companies and distributors. As I read this all back, it sounds overwhelming. So much to do! How did I know where to start? I was lucky to have an investor who believed in me and could show me the ropes, but while it was happening, it was just one foot in front of the other. It was like hiking Runyon Canyon: I'd think, *OMG, I'm finally done!*—but nope, I had to keep going. I just kept reminding myself that other people had done this, so I could, too. I had no idea what the formula was for launching a business, yet somehow, by taking it one step at a time, I was doing it.

ENJOY THE PINCH-ME MOMENTS

Because I was always laser-focused on whatever task was directly in front of me, it was hard to appreciate what I was accomplishing as I began to build the company. There were little moments—walking through an aerosol lab or meeting with fragrance creators—where I had to remind myself that this was real, but I didn't want to get ahead of myself. I didn't want to get too excited until I knew, for sure, that my dream was really happening.

Even still, there were a couple of *holy shit* moments. The day I walked into our first WeWork office blew my mind. By then we had eight or nine employees, and this company I'd started in my living room finally had an actual space, with desks and conference rooms and gorgeous hair shots adorning the walls. There was our initial sales meeting with Sephora where we pitched them on carrying OUAI in their stores. I only had sketches to share, because we didn't have physical products yet, but I sat down with the head buyer and gave her my whole spiel: *This is who I am, here's what I think is missing, here's what I came up with.* And she offered to take our products on the spot, which I absolutely did not see coming. That was the first time I let myself think, *This might actually take off.*

Then there was the day we launched. I'll never forget walking into the giant Sephora at the Grove in L.A., which is basically a sprawling outdoor shopping mall, and seeing our product out in the world . . . and also my own face hanging on a store display. I mean, what?!? That kind of thing happened to my clients, not to me. And honestly? It was exciting but also scary—I felt really, really vulnerable. But I was proud, and I was optimistic. February 1, 2016, was a day full of tears. So many of my friends had shown up for me, posting about OUAI on their coveted Instagram grid, Twitter, or Snaps, and I could tell almost immediately, at least on social, that something special was happening. It was so encouraging, because no matter how much you believe in a brand or a product, you never know what's going to happen when it's released into the world. Sure, you can have a gut feeling, and I like to think that after years in this business my intuition is pretty good. But not always.

Our wave spray, for example, was one of our earliest big hits, and I felt that one coming in my bones. It was the first wave spray on the market that didn't contain alcohol, which meant it never got sticky but it still helped build up the hair, whether you were air-drying or blow-drying. But we've had some duds that I would have sworn were going to take off. Like our after-sun soother. I thought it was going to be major—the foam made an ASMR sound* and had aloe in it, and it felt so good on sunburned skin. But it never took off, and the customer reviews were variations on "Why would I buy this for twenty bucks when I could just go to CVS and get some aloe for $5?" *Huh. I hadn't thought of that.*

Now our team is able to have a laugh at the products that didn't work out. When we read the negative reviews of our first take on dry shampoo on OUAI's YouTube channel, we had a little failure party that served as a real team builder. My point is, there's not a ton of glamour in the early days of business-building. The work is never done, and there are countless missteps, so anytime you find yourself doing that internal squeal, thinking, *Holy shit, is this really happening?*, just stop and take a minute to appreciate it. Those moments don't come around all that often.

PAY IT FORWARD

Crafting a business philosophy is about more than just articulating what paid goods or services you will offer. You also have to think through what you want to stand for as an organization. When we started OUAI, there weren't many companies who would take a stance on political and social issues. But I think as people grew less trusting of

---

* *For the uninitiated, ASMR (autonomous sensory meridian response) is the soothing, tingly feeling you get—usually in the back of your head and spine—when listening to certain comforting sounds. Check out the zillions of YouTube ASMR videos and you'll get why we thought we were onto something.*

politicians (ahem, Trump), they became increasingly interested in the opinions of leaders and brands in the private sector. So ask yourself: What is your company's place in the world? How will you integrate into the larger industry you belong to? Giving back was built into the OUAI ethos from the beginning. Mormons put aside 10 percent of their earnings in a tradition known as tithing—kind of like a communal tax you pay in order to help others and support the church—so giving back was drilled into me from my earliest churchgoing days. Grandpa Atkin took his kids on trips to perform acts of service in the communities they visited, and I can't wait to pass the tradition on to my own kids one day. My parents took us to Mexico and Alaska and Las Vegas, and all that exposure to other cultures taught me that there was a world beyond our bubble.* I saw that there were good people everywhere, and I learned how to connect with people from different cultures with different belief systems. We were always going out of our comfort zone, and it made me realize how big the world is. It also taught me that I was just one small piece in the universe's much larger puzzle, which is why I feel it's so important that my companies do their part to serve the community at large. I always saw the family volunteer work that Mormons are known for as more of a social obligation than a religious one.

At OUAI, we've partnered with organizations like Period.org, March for Our Lives, She's the First, Women for Women International, Black Lives Matter, NAACP, the LA

---

* *Don't laugh, there's culture in Las Vegas.*

LGBTQ Center, and Vanderpump Dogs* in hopes of raising awareness and raising funds. We donate money or pro-
ceeds of profits, or volunteer our time, in our own version
of tithing. At Mane Addicts, we do Give Back Days every
quarter, pairing up with organizations like Baby2Baby and
apps like H.E.L.P. We also work with nonprofits that help
abused women, kids in foster homes, and survivors of sex
trafficking, by bringing in hairstylists who donate their
time to pamper the women and girls these nonprofits serve.

Donating money or time, or doing Give Back Days is
pretty easy for my companies, because we have money coming in and we have relationships with salons that can donate space and stylists who can volunteer time. But I'm a
huge believer in doing what you can, and that's true for
whatever business you might launch one day. Get clear on
the kind of business you want to be and the type of culture
you want to create from the beginning, because weaving
those intentions into the fabric of your company will help
make it easier to put them into practice when your skyrocketing success has you running in ten different directions.

I can honestly say that the entire OUAI team takes
our commitment to service seriously, and that throughout the company, employees are taking action, learning,
and growing all the time as human beings and citizens.
When I say we have our ear to the ground, I'm not just
talking about products. I'm talking about social and political concerns. One lesson I learned as a female founder after
George Floyd's death was to not get stuck in the lane of

---

* *Yes, that Vanderpump. Lisa and Ken created this rescue organization
after seeing a legit dog meat festival in China.*

fighting only for female equality and sending the elevator back down for other women but also for intersectionality. It's critical to create opportunities for BIPOC, LGBTQ, and other discriminated groups of people as you build your path to success. Recognize your privilege and raise awareness. Question inequality at work, school, and in your personal life. The only way my female founder friends and I found success was with the help of allies.

YOUR INNER BOSS BITCH

No one is more surprised at my "businesswoman" title than I am. I could never have envisioned where OUAI is today, especially not when that first kernel of an idea for a hair-care line popped into my head. But today, while I obviously adore my clients, and Mane Addicts is near and dear to my heart (it's basically my firstborn), OUAI, for now, is my professional identity. Creating a CPG company* means putting yourself and your ideas out there in the most terrifying way possible. People are either going to say "yes this has value, and I'm going to allocate some of my hard-earned money to it" or . . . they're not. And if they don't, you may not stay in business. It's super-scary, but I can't even begin to explain how rewarding it is when it works. For me, ratcheting up the nerve to launch a business meant putting my money where my mouth was. Literally, because I had to put all of my own and my husband's savings into the business—but also figuratively, because I had

* *CPG = consumer packaged goods.*

to draw on all the risk-taking and confidence-building and professionalism and hustling that I've written about thus far. And not to sound like your annoying big sister, but if I could learn how to create a business, you can, too. Tell that pesky voice in your head—the one saying "I wouldn't know where to start" or "It sounds like too much work" or "I'm not a businessperson" or "I'm not smart enough"—to shut up, and pump up the volume on those whispers of "I think I'm onto something big." Channel your inner boss bitch, sit your butt in front of your computer, and ask yourself those three very powerful words: Why not me?

Just a few of my Post-its I write goals on—2018

CHAPTER SIX
SETTING
INTENTIONS . . .
AND CHANGING
YOUR MIND

S etting goals is in the Mormon DNA. From the moment I could write I was encouraged to keep a diary, document my life plans, and keep track of my accomplishments. My childhood home was basically where gold-star stickers went to die—each of us had a chart of goals for the week that hung on the fridge for the rest of us to see. Accomplish what you set out to do? Gold star for you! If not . . . well, everyone could see your empty square on the chart, which meant that there was real pressure to achieve, or even overachieve. Our directive was clear: keep busy and enroll in extracurriculars and pursue your passions.*

My goals have changed countless times over the past

---

* Of course, not all passions were created equal. Reading the Bible or singing or playing an instrument or sports = good. Steamy backseat make-out sesh, aka "heavy petting" = not so much.

twenty years, and they will change plenty more down the road. When I started working at a salon, my goals were pretty simple: nail the beachy waves, live a happy life, and do good work. I think those are pretty honorable goals— and I can say now that I really did achieve them. I may not be happy every single moment of every single day, but I am a happy person. And I'm proud of the work I do. But I'm also a bit of an overachiever who loves to try new things, so as soon as I was lucky enough to achieve those goals, I started wondering about what else I could do, and what else after that. I guess you could say I've been setting new intentions and testing my limits my entire life.

WRITE IT DOWN

Given my fondness for documenting content—from the diaries, lists, and scrapbooks of my childhood to the spreadsheets, journals, and Insta captions of my adult years—it should come as no surprise that I'm a big-time believer in writing down goals. Putting intentions on paper helps me prioritize my hopes and dreams and see the big picture—and also, eventually, to reflect on how far I've come (or, alternatively, how little progress I've made, which is equally important to acknowledge).

I carve out time to work on goal-setting at the beginning of each year, and I'm pretty methodical about it. I write down up to three goals in each of six different categories: personal, health, career, financial, recreational, and spiritual. Then I make a separate, bigger-picture list of what I want to have, who I want to be, and what I want do over the next six months. Then I create a sublist of the actions I'll take to achieve those goals. After six months have passed, I review both lists to check in on my progress.

If I lost you at "six different categories," never fear: It sounds more complicated than it is, I promise. To help you get a better sense of how this works, here's an example of what my goal list looked like in 2016:

PERSONAL: Get a dog, buy a house, kids???

HEALTH: Eat better, start running again, go back to yoga and Pilates

CAREER: Launch a hair-care line, manage salon schedule better, staff Mane Addicts

FINANCIAL: Pay better attention to savings

RECREATIONAL: Travel to South America, Turkey *(note: I still haven't done either)*

SPIRITUAL: Get more sleep, take time to meditate, continue to keep charitable causes in the schedule

HAVE: A puppy!

BE: Less stressed

DO: Drink less alcohol, read more business books, do more charitable work

I keep my annual goal lists together in a single notebook so that I can easily get a snapshot of the bigger picture.

GOAL PLANNING

Every year, I ask myself: What would I be, have, and do if failure were not an option? Then I write down up to three goals in each of six categories: personal, health, career, financial, recreational, and spiritual. I think about these goals in six-month installments, and reevaluate when those six months have passed. This template is here to help you set goals to create the life and career you deserve. Your best life starts NOW!

IF FAILURE WERE NOT AN OPTION, WHAT WOULD I...

HAVE:

Steps to achieve this:

1.

2.

3.

BE:

Steps to achieve this:

1.

2.

3.

DO:

Steps to achieve this:

1.

2.

3.

GOALS (up to 3)

PERSONAL:

HEALTH:

CAREER:

FINANCIAL:

RECREATIONAL:

SPIRITUAL:

Sometimes I get to check items off; other times I'm reminded that I need to rearrange my schedule if I want to achieve a goal by year's end. I may look at some goals and think, *No, that's not important to me anymore*, and others might suddenly seem completely unrealistic. (In 2019 I wrote, "500k YouTube subscribers by 2020." Six months in, I only had 110,000, because apparently no one had told me how hard it is to grow on YouTube.) When it's time to check in and reflect, it gives me a boost to look back and see all the hard work it took to get some big wins. It's easy to lose track of what you've accomplished on a larger scale when you're distracted by day-to-day life. And it's even easier to get so focused on what you *haven't* achieved that you forget to acknowledge the victories along the way.

Plenty of people might argue for starting with a clean slate each year rather than keeping the annual lists together in one place, but the ability to look back at multiple years at a time is a wonderful way to identify patterns in your own behavior or mental state. Case in point: I wrote "drink less" on my list in 2016, 2017, and 2018, and each of those years I also listed "be less stressed." I finally cut out alcohol for good in 2018, and looking back now, it's so obvious that I was drinking to quiet my mind and take the edge off my anxiety. Had I realized that earlier, of course, it could have saved me a lot of hassle—and money on wine. But it became obvious that when I finally conquered one goal (better stress management), I was able to conquer the other (quit drinking). And—bonus!—I also stopped waking up feeling drained and looking as dehydrated as a raisin.

Writing down my goals has always been a great kick in

the pants to take action and stay motivated. But setting intentions isn't a one-and-done kind of thing. It's a constant ebb and flow—there's always something more you may want to accomplish, and there's always something else that will pop up and muddy the plan. You can't control every situation, so you have to learn to cope with that frustration and disappointment. That's why I include up to three goals on each list—I know I'll never cross off all of them, but if I can check off one item in each category I'll feel good. (I told you I was raised in the land of gold stars! There are certain things a girl just can't shake.)

For some people, six months may seem like too grand a plan. I've gone through phases of my life where just getting through the day felt like an accomplishment, so maybe you start with daily check-ins based on smaller, achievable goals. Or weekly check-ins, if that makes more sense for where you are right now. You can break it into any time increment you want—the important thing is that these goals should help you feel more in control of your life.

Whatever time frame you choose, I can't stress this enough: write down *all* the goals, even if they seem big and unattainable. The worst-case scenario is that you don't achieve them and THAT IS OKAY. But maybe you'll take a small step in the right direction. The fact that I can look back at that 2016 list, with its very ambitious goal to "launch a hair-care line," and know that OMG, WE DID IT! . . . it's pretty damn satisfying. (Also, look up the video for Chris Martin manifesting Coldplay's fame like thirty years ago—it's a good mood booster.)

GOALS SHOULD ENRICH YOUR LIFE, NOT LIMIT IT

I have no intention of telling anyone what their goals should be—the most beautiful journeys are the unexpected ones that people create for themselves—but I wholeheartedly believe that whatever your dreams, they should be about expanding who you are rather than fitting into someone else's vision of who you should be. Trying to better yourself is one thing, but if you're fixated on getting richer or more popular or skinnier, you're in dangerous territory. We live in a world where everyone wants validation; everyone wants to be envied or admired. But there's a happy medium between being a role model and getting caught up in a superficial, image-conscious existence.

When you sit down to think about your intentions for the coming week/month/year/decade, give yourself a minute to take stock of what's driving you. Do you feel a deep sense of yearning, as if achieving your goal will help you finally become the person you were meant to be? Do you crave the feeling of independence and self-sufficiency, the way I did when I was in hair school and I was just dying to get on the salon floor and prove my skills? Or are your goals focused more on attaining things that may not actually matter much to you, but you think *should* matter to you because everyone else seems to have them? This latter drive is a real recipe for disaster—when your priorities are based on keeping up with the Joneses, nothing will ever be enough. The minute you hit one goal, you'll find somewhere else you fall short. If you're focused on having the same body as your friends, once you get there you'll wish you had their clothes or car. If all you care about is more social media followers, as soon as you hit 100,000 you'll wonder why you don't have more partnership offers. Ever heard the expression "do what you love and the money will follow"? I absolutely subscribe to that. Focusing on what you don't have—or what other people do have—is a trap that is guaranteed to keep you down, and the purpose of goal-setting is to help you rise up.

Just as your goals shouldn't limit your happiness, I often caution my assistants that they shouldn't let their goals get too far ahead of the opportunities in front of them, either. What I mean by that is, don't let some far-off ambition distract from the amazing possibilities before you right now. I've seen so many artists who've had their minds set on styling a particular celebrity client, for example, when in reality the chance of actually working with that person was really slim. Their focus—or even obsession—with working with that person *at some point* became a distraction, and they never truly appreciated the amazing place they'd gotten to or the amazing clients they did have in the moment. Their ambition became counterproductive, and of course that can happen to anyone, in any field. Maybe you're launching a business and you dream of partnering with a major brand, so you overlook the smaller collabs that other people would kill for. Maybe you're a writer who dreams of seeing your byline in the *New York Times*, so you don't promote your smaller assignments, even though they're helping to build the portfolio you need. Maybe you're a lawyer with dreams of arguing in front of the Supreme Court, so nothing else feels impressive enough. My point is this: dream big, but don't let your pie-in-the-sky, long-term goals diminish the value of your incremental accomplishments. You want to find that delicate balance between aiming for the stars and concentrating on life here on earth.

KNOW WHEN TO CHANGE COURSE

Here's a simple fact that society doesn't tell us nearly enough: It's okay to change your mind. People change. Values change. Interests, passions, circumstances, priorities—all of these things evolve over time, and that's completely normal and expected and acceptable. As with my kick-ass assistants who decided to leave L.A. for a different kind of life, sometimes being happy might mean doing what you love in a different context than you'd initially imagined. Other times it could mean letting go of a dream entirely. Starting in childhood, we are inundated with messages like "follow your dreams!" and "don't give up!" and, sure, I believe in those mantras—my feed is full of them—but they come at the risk of pressuring people into sticking with decisions or staying in lifestyles that may no longer serve them. It's completely okay if your dream at twenty-eight isn't the same as it was when you were eighteen, and revising your vision board doesn't make you a quitter.* Revisiting my own goals every six months isn't just an exercise in evaluating my accomplishments, it's also an opportunity to reevaluate my priorities. Old dreams may fade, but entirely new dreams can emerge, too. I mean, social media didn't even exist when I was a teenager! I couldn't have dreamed that in twenty-five years there would be a platform where I could interact with 3 million people a day or crowdsource business and product ideas. The whole thing would have sounded completely insane to my fifteen-year-old self. But here we are. So don't forget, the secret ingredient that could help drive your success might not even exist yet—who knows what will happen in the next ten years.†

I'm so grateful that I was able to start a business in this era of digital innovation, but it doesn't seem crazy to me at all to imagine that the thing that could help bring *your* career to the next level might, as you're reading this, be nothing more than an idea in someone's head. Isn't that exciting? As you progress on your path, make sure you don't get so totally tunnel-visioned on one way of doing things that you don't see what other avenues emerge over time. You risk missing some incredible opportunities, so keep your eyes and ears open.

---

* *I like to remind my clients that age twenty-seven is your return to Saturn—basically when the planet returns to where it was when you were born. It's an internal cue that you need to grow up. To that end, your late twenties and early thirties are usually when you figure out what you want to do with your life. It's an empowering time when you gain confidence and stop caring as much what other people think, so it makes sense that you might have a shift in your #GOALS.*

† **Smokes weed and imagines our Jetsons-like future**

Another unfortunate truth that I've learned firsthand is that sometimes when you achieve your dreams, they look a little different than you'd imagined. So much of my career—of my life, really—has been motivated by the desire for freedom. I left home in order to pursue an existence that would allow me to do work that feels good and make choices that feel right for me. But now that I've started a successful business and I'm the face of a brand, my choices are more restricted. Anytime I want to do something new, it needs to be approved by a team of people. These days I sign a zillion contracts and have noncompete clauses and I have to navigate a world where I can't post certain content or can't say yes to certain opportunities because they might conflict with others (there's that noncompete clause at work!). It's complicated and sometimes frustrating for me to deal with all of these checks and balances on my freedom. Don't get me wrong—I'm tremendously grateful for the career I have, but I'm not entirely sure I understood what I was getting into when I set off on my own. I've definitely lost some freedom in the name of building a successful business, and that's been hard for me to swallow at times. I want to be honest about it here, because I don't want any of my advice to mislead you—especially those of you who have a strong entrepreneurial drive. Creating your own business is a wonderful thing, but if your goals include things like "be independent" or "be my own boss," there may be a few surprises in store for you. Everything comes with a price, and rules, attached.

And since we're talking hard truths, there's one more reason you might find yourself wanting to change course: not all dreams come to fruition. There's nothing shameful about that, and I'm sure plenty of businesspeople with way more experience than I have would say that if you've never fallen short of a goal, you aren't aiming high enough. As was the case with the blow-dry bar I tried to launch before OUAI, some dreams never take off, and you have to be okay with accepting that loss and moving on. You have to have the confidence in yourself to know that just because one thing didn't work out, that doesn't mean your next project won't be a huge hit. I've learned that when things don't go as planned, it's important to take stock of what went wrong (which could be anything from a flawed idea to a flawed team to flawed communication to simple bad luck or bad timing) and, using that knowledge, chart a new course—I believe Silicon Valley calls this "pivoting." The ability to recover without totally giving up is probably the most valuable business skill of all.

My own road map has changed countless times, but if I think back on all the dreams I had for my life, my biggest surprise "fail" wasn't professional but personal. When I was young, I had zero interest in marriage. I hated the idea of someone taking away my freedom, and I thought that a ring represented a superficial and unrealistic ideal, which is funny considering that my parents have been happily married for more than forty years. If you asked anyone who knew me in my twenties, they would tell you that Jen Atkin would never, ever get married. No way, nohow.

When Mike surprised me with a beautiful ring one day, I was floored. And not in that "oh my gosh, you swept me off my feet!" kind of way. I was speechless, and I definitely left him hanging for a few minutes. We'd been dating for five years and had never discussed marriage even once. I had a momentary freak-out when I saw him down on one knee—*this is not the plan!*, I thought—but what I actually said was "Yes, if you promise we don't have to have a wedding." My life plan may have changed in an instant, but no one was going to get me into a fluffy white dress.

Today, of course, I couldn't be more grateful that I failed to meet my goal of staying single. The relationship I'm in is nothing like the one I was avoiding—it's a true partnership that expands my life rather than limiting it. I'm so happy I recognized an incredible thing when I saw it and that I was willing to revise my vision . . . even if it did mean enduring a lot of "I told you so"s from my friends.

LEAPING LILY PADS

When people discuss their career goals, they usually talk about climbing a ladder, but I've never especially liked that metaphor. I don't love the idea of climbing straight up, because then you can't take a step sideways and change paths—and it also means that eventually you might hit a ceiling. In the real world, there is no final destination. You can always grow more and learn more and find fulfillment in different places. A professional or personal evolution should look like jumping from lily pad to lily pad, because life might throw shit that will sideswipe you, but then you'll just land on the lily pad a little to the left. It makes for a more interesting and less predictable career . . . and journey.

Before you take this as permission to hop from one job to the next from month to month, remember that a resume with, say, five jobs in three years is usually a red flag for any recruiter or hiring manager. It is entirely possible to jump around and take a circuitous route while still giving ample time and dedication to each commitment you make. When I interview candidates at Mane Addicts or OUAI and I see that someone has had multiple jobs in the last six months, my takeaway is that they're easily distracted every time something shiny and new comes along, or that they're too focused on their far-off dream job to do the job they have now. Dreams are great, but you also have to put in the time to master a skill set before you can grow—and loyalty is valuable. The assistants I reward are the ones who aren't constantly looking for the next best thing. They're focused and not afraid to dive into the work, and they always see their projects through. Everyone is allowed a blip on their resume, but if there's a clear pattern of moving on as soon as the going gets tough (because the first few months are orientation, and things don't get real until you've truly settled in), that tells me you don't have what it takes to be on my team.

One thing I hear a lot from my followers is that while they like their current job and they know they have more to learn, they're not getting the salary or job title they feel they're entitled to. *How do I get a promotion?* they ask. *How do I get a raise?* There's no easy answer to either of these questions, but I do think it's important to consider that when it comes to growth within a company, your performance isn't the only factor for your employer. If you haven't gotten a salary or title bump in a while, it might be that your boss is focused on trying to keep the business afloat (and therefore preserve your job), that budgets are tight, or that there just isn't a lot of room for growth within that particular organization. I know this doesn't offer much solace, but hopefully it serves as a reminder to take your future into your own hands. Instead of waiting for the offer you think you deserve, be proactive and go get it. Write down a list of your successes, and collect data that proves your value. Did you work on a project that generated a huge social following? Did you contribute to a product that brought in tons of revenue? Did you successfully navigate a partnership that involved coordinating dozens of people? Do clients love working with you and request you for their projects? Arm yourself with examples to back up *why* you deserve more money or responsibility. Present the proof that you've gone above and beyond. And then be clear about your goals to continue to help the company grow. A raise or a promotion is as much about the commitment you're making to perform for your company as it is about your company recognizing the value of what you've already done. It's not just a reward for sitting at your desk and putting in the hours. So gather your evidence and come prepared. And if the conversation doesn't go the way you'd hoped, well, remember that the next lily pad isn't so far off.

THE POWER OF POSITIVE THINKING

As human beings, it's second nature for us to become distracted by our fears. It goes back to when we were cavemen running from tigers—survival was key. Of course, in those days it was about literal survival. Today we've evolved far past that, and yet those fight-or-flight instincts are still hardwired in us. When faced with something scary—and now that's usually a tough obstacle or the potential for failure rather than an actual life-threatening event—we run in the opposite direction. Self-preservation is important, but when it causes an aversion to facing our fears, it can also keep us from realizing our goals. Positive thinking is an antidote to this attitude. It can be the thing that shifts your outlook from "too hard, unsubscribe" to "if they can do it, so can I." And, believe me, I know this isn't easy. I constantly have to remind myself to think positively—and I'm a glass-half-full kind of girl.

Even on my best days, sometimes I hear that annoying voice telling me, *This is too difficult* or *You can't do that* or *You're an impostor.* Impostor syndrome, that nagging feeling that you don't deserve your success or that you don't actually know what you're doing, and the accompanying fear that you will one day be "found out," is very real and very common. Especially in women. I mean, even Tina Fey has admitted to it! But no matter how much you fear that you're not cut out for whatever challenge is before you, you need to resist the urge to tear yourself down. Focusing on negative thoughts will only produce negative results. I want to acknowledge that this is harder if you're a victim of abuse, racism, homophobia, or discrimination. If you've experienced trauma, please don't be embarrassed to seek help, and don't feel like you have to go it alone. Acknowledging what's taken place is healing; you're not responsible for your reality and didn't deserve to experience it.

When I start to feel those second-guessing fears creep in, I know that a large part of what keeps me moving forward is shifting my focus to a positive place where I'm not just focused on the goal I'm pursuing but also on the belief that I'm going to reach it. Acknowledge the fear or negativity, then let it go. It's okay to feel insecure, and it's normal to think through worst-case scenarios, but you can't let self-doubt become your baseline and dominate your headspace. It's easy to default to being cynical, but with practice, it's just as easy for your brain to default to a more open and productive mindset. One simple way to shift your thinking is to focus on gratitude. You might list five things you're thankful for each day. Or maybe you write one daily note of appreciation to a person who did something nice for you. Start off with the basics: your family, health, friends, roof over your head, and so on. Maybe take a minute before bed to remember something good that happened to you that day. Think about one thing you're looking forward to tomorrow. Write it down to reinforce it in your mind, or maybe even say it aloud to put those thoughts out into the universe.

I've mentioned that I'm not really one for prayer, but I believe, 100 percent, that our thoughts hold a lot of power. If you set intentions for your life but deep down believe your goals are too big or that you're not capable of achieving them, you're undermining yourself. Make yourself a vision board.* Meditate while reciting inspiring mantras.

---

* Real Talk: "Vision board" is just a fancy name for those collages we all made as teenagers, with magazine cutouts of houses we wanted to live in one day or places we wanted to travel. Find images or words that represent your intentions or the life you want and put them on a poster that you can look at when you need a reminder of what all the hard work is for. There! You just manifested your destiny.

Stand in front of the bathroom mirror and give yourself a pep talk. Practice shifting your thoughts to a more positive, less fear-based place. It's not easy at first, especially when you feel like you're drowning in daily responsibilities, but over time it will become a reflex. Invest the time; you and your goals are worth it.

My first luggage collab with Calpak—2018

BTS of the cover shoot for *WWD Beauty Inc.*
with the women in my life who help me keep
it all together—2018

CHAPTER SEVEN
ALL THE LADIES

I've been a feminist since before I knew what a feminist was. What I did know, as a kid, was that I lived in a community where my church taught me one thing but I felt another. As a young girl, the message delivered to me was that women were valued less than their husbands. They were not allowed to hold the priesthood or bless their children like their husbands could or hold other important roles within the church, and in my family, while my mother worked inside and outside the home, my father controlled the finances (which was also typical for their generation, Mormon or not). I remember as a teenager looking around at the women in my neighborhood who spent all day and night caring for their children and running a household, and it made zero sense to me that they didn't get a paycheck like their husbands did. Cooking and cleaning and caretaking was obviously a majorly stressful job, and I couldn't understand why women—always women—were expected to do it for free.

As high school progressed and my classmates and I became increasingly curious about sex, the church went hard on the importance of remaining a virgin; we were taught abstinence rather than contraception, and I remember being warned that I wouldn't be able to find a husband if I didn't remain "pure." The idea that my virginity alone would qualify me as being worthy of a man never sat right with me, not to mention the unsettling fact that women weren't allowed to decide when to start a family or how. I'm not trying to bash the Mormon Church here—my whole family is made up of practicing Mormons. I have a lot of respect for people who find solace in any religion, but some of the traditional male/female roles that I was taught by my church just never felt like a fit with what I've always believed to be true. I was also perplexed that they didn't allow Black members of the church until the late 1970s. And don't get me started on their stance on LGBTQ people.

While I've thought about feminist issues since I was a kid, I've given them more practical consideration as I've established a career and built a business. It's crazy to me that we like to think we've come so far as a society, and yet obvious inequalities continue to persist. As a teenager, I didn't want to accept the fact that women weren't given the same opportunities and weren't paid the same wages, but I couldn't put a name to those feelings, so I just kept a chip on my shoulder. Now, as a card-carrying feminist, I think a lot about how I, as a businessWOMAN, can integrate *my* values into the workplaces I've established. I've made an effort to do this from the beginning, but, full disclosure, I didn't always walk the walk. It's easy to call yourself a #feminist on social media, but what does it look like to support other women in real life, especially in business? I learned this the hard way, and it took way too long, but I'm so glad I finally figured it out.

A MAN'S WORLD

Historically, hairdressing has been a man's game. When I was working at Estilo and The Chris McMillan Salon and watching the stylists in action, I rarely saw a woman haircutter who was as busy as the guys were. That wasn't because men are innately better at doing hair, obviously, but because, as with most industries, hairstyling was male-dominated, and it was hard to break into the boys' club. When I was growing up, and even into my late teens, the only women in the hair business with any mainstream name recognition were Sally Hershberger and Odile Gilbert. And even though these women were able to create successful businesses, I can't imagine how much shit they had to deal with just to earn a fraction of the respect (and money) that the men in their field did. To this day, I owe a debt of gratitude to Sally and Odile for paving the way for stylists like me.

When I finally got my own chair on the salon floor in 2006, I didn't have a female hairdresser to serve as a mentor. I had to develop my own game plan for surviving and thriving in the hair club for men, and after years of refining my approach, I feel pretty strongly that it works no matter what male-dominated industry you're in (which is to say, any industry).*

---

* *I should add that I really hate the phrase "male-dominated." It's so intense and aggressive—it freaks me out, as if men are swarming around in packs and trying to exert their power over women everywhere they go. I don't think the world is quite like that—at least not usually—and I'm not advocating that women embark on any sort of hostile takeover. But we deserve to be treated equally.*

The first and most important rule: hone your talent. Get really, really good at whatever it is you do, because you're probably going to have to be twice as good as the guy standing next to you. (I pray that this changes over time.) You want your skill to speak for itself so that if you're passed over for a job or offered different opportunities or compensation than a man, no one can get away with blaming it on your ability. Read. Learn. Watch videos, attend seminars. Put in the time.

And while you're honing your skills, make it a priority to seek out a mentor. Ideally this person would be female, but if female mentors are hard to come by in your industry, just find someone, anyone, who believes in you. When she or he offers guidance and feedback, accept the help with gratitude. Look for opportunities to connect with people you can learn from and collaborate with at all levels, too— the notion of being stronger together is very true. Find allies and join forces. Once you have a squad, you're better positioned to change the work environment and create spaces for everyone.

But here's the thing: if you succeed in busting through the barriers that were created to keep you out, you have a responsibility to help the people who come after you make it through, too. This is where I fell short when my career was starting to take off. As soon as I had the opportunity to hire assistants, I hired men and more men. There I was, trying to break the stigma that only guys could be successful stylists, but I wasn't bringing women up with me. I think subconsciously I'd bought into the myth that young women would make for emotional employees. I believed on some level that a man might be more dedicated to his work. (I know, I know. I'm not proud of this. But the roots of patriarchy are deep, and it takes a while to dismantle all of these biases. I continue to work on unlearning them every day.) I also knew that the job required significant physical strength, because we have to carry around a lot of heavy things—I knew this because *I, a woman, had done the job and carried heavy things*—and I thought a man might have an easier time with the physical part. It was so stupid, and I was so wrong. To this day, my biggest career regret is not hiring women sooner.

I *am* proud to say, however, that I saw the error of my ways and course corrected accordingly. In 2014, I hired my first female assistant, Justine. At the time, I was starting to travel to the Middle East more often and I needed more women on my team—I worked mostly in salons or wedding suites, where men weren't allowed because the women weren't fully covered. So I hired Justine, and then two more talented stylists, Carly and Alex, and then Irinel and Amanda, and everything changed. I don't think it's a coincidence that around this time my business really started to flourish. Mane Addicts took off and my client list grew, and that was thanks to these ladies—they multitasked like I've never seen, and they learned fast. I was clear about my confidence in them, and they reflected it right back to me with excellent work. In fact, my own ability to multitask improved, because they were running circles around me. Of course, this isn't to say that men aren't also capable assistants—of course they are. But I am embarrassed that it took me so long to give these women a chance.

And then, a little less than four years after I hired my amazing team of young women, Donald Trump was elected president of the United States.

I was devastated, and, like so many women, I went through a pretty hard time trying to understand what had happened. But there was a silver lining—in the backlash against his victory, the support for female-founded companies and the call for female empowerment in general got really loud. My female employees and I banded together at a time when the spotlight was shining bright on businesses like ours. We needed each other, and we all delivered. To date, between OUAI and Mane Addicts, we have about sixty employees—and nearly 88 percent of them are women.

That said, I still have work to do when it comes to diversifying my workplace. I regret that I didn't take the time earlier to make sure there was enough representation around me for LGBTQ, BIPOC, and disabled people. I was so caught up in creating opportunities for women that I wasn't doing everything I could to expand the diversity on my teams. It's so important to do that work internally. Examining corporate policies, hiring processes, and diversity initiatives should always be top of mind. These efforts should be ongoing. Truly, nothing feels better than creating opportunity for those who have to fight for it.

The hairstyling industry is much more equitable today than it was when I started out, and that evolution has been truly amazing to watch. The success rate of women in salons and celebrity glam and editorial styling is unprecedented. Social media has been especially instrumental in the rise of women in my industry, and I really believe it's helped to level the playing field. Why? Because connecting with our communities and sharing information comes naturally to us. If we try a product we love, we take a pic and post. Yes, I realize this is a huge generalization, and there are plenty of fantastic male content creators out there, but most women I know have an instinct to share and connect, while I don't think men have historically been raised with that mentality. In an era when businesses are increasingly being built on social communities, I think that offers us an advantage.*

LET ME CLEAR MY THROAT

The biggest lesson I learned from my own hiring missteps is that feminism is so much more than just believing in equality or posting about the issues you care about. Putting feminist values into action means using your voice to advocate for yourself *and* for the women or other marginalized groups that could use your help.

Finding (and using) your voice is an ever-evolving process. Each time you speak up is a victory, but inevitably another moment arises —and once again, you'll need to help someone understand the value you bring to the table. Maybe you want to start a business or get a bank loan or be considered for a leadership role on a project. Maybe you want a promotion or a salary increase, or you want to hire or promote a talented team member. Each time, someone will need convincing.

Of course, when I talk about using your voice, I'm not

---

* **Insert Nancy Pelosi clapping GIF here.**

referring strictly to speaking—there are lots of ways to make your opinions known. Social media can be a powerful platform. When people talk about activism of any sort in reference to social media, it's often met with eye rolls about "thoughts and prayers"—in other words, all talk, no action. But as we've seen during many major world events, social networks provide real opportunities to lift each other up. Even in the wake of a pandemic, we saw a historic number of protestors take to the streets in support of social movements—moving their activism offline and into the real world. Social media has given us a microphone and a platform and an opportunity to raise awareness; it has afforded us the ability to connect and cross-promote and dispel the ridiculous yet pervasive myth in our culture that women are constantly in competition, always trying to tear each other down. I mean, it's straight out of the patriarchy playbook: *Uh-oh, women invest in relationships and find strength in numbers and build communities rather than trying to yell over each other and be the loudest voice in the room . . . let's turn them against each other to limit their power.* No effing way am I falling into that trap.

In another attempt to squash the whole "catty competitive women" trope, I find myself on the phone, at least once a week, with someone from a glam squad who wants to start a brand. Honestly, it's one of the hardest parts about running a business—you forget how much extra time you need to slot in for those informational phone calls. But doing so is essential if you want to pass the torch. I also make a point to support female-owned and Black-female-owned businesses. This is vital, because money talks—we can't keep women in business if we don't give them our business! But you can also think smaller-scale. Help one young girl improve her self-image or find her confidence or understand her ability to speak up for herself. If you have a daughter or sister, plant the seed for her now that she has a voice worth using, even if that means enabling her to question the very values that you hold dear. I get DMs all the time from young kids in small towns in Utah who are struggling in the same ways I did, and I offer them support, but I also encourage them to support those around them. The only way to make change in a society that undervalues certain groups is to find your collective power. My hope is that everyone, in all industries and all communities, will know that nothing can change if we don't find a way to band together. Once we all start to use our voices to demand policy changes, vote, and live the values that we espouse in hashtags, that's when progress will really start to happen.

INVEST IN YOUR GIRLGANG

For the first five years I lived in L.A., maybe even more, the idea of starting a business was nowhere on my radar. It wasn't even in my orbit. Then, suddenly, it seemed like I was surrounded by girlfriends launching entrepreneurial endeavors. During the workday, I was hustling in the salon and styling celebrity clients (many of whom were also dreaming of brand-building outside of entertainment), and after-hours, I'd dish with my friends about our wildest ambitions—dreams that seemed exciting but totally impossible. But as time passed, more and more of the women around me decided to give their big ideas a shot. It was as if everyone was throwing spaghetti at a wall, trying their hand at one idea and then the next. It was so inspiring to watch. Instead of just talking about what they wished they could do, these women were out there *doing* it.

And while not everyone's idea worked out, there were plenty of successes—many of which you probably know about, because these ladies hit it *big*. Hillary Kerr and Katherine Power started WhoWhatWear, and Sophia Rossi started Hello Giggles. Sophia Amoruso launched Nasty Gal. Emily Weiss launched Glossier from her blog, *Into the Gloss*, and Huda and Mona Kattan launched Huda Beauty. Kim launched KKW Beauty and Skims, Chrissy Teigen launched Cravings, Jessica Alba launched Honest, Anastasia expanded her empire, Khloé launched Good American, and Kylie launched Kylie Cosmetics. I was just standing by, totally in awe of all of them. They were innovative and scrappy and believed in disrupting industries. Hillary and Katherine would film videos for the website in Katherine's closet—they understood back in 2005 that editorial was going to shift from print to digital, and that there wasn't anything in the online fashion space like what they were offering. (I went to their website every morning and checked out the collages for outfit inspo.) During those years, as I was starting to think about the kind of business I wanted to build, my social life basically consisted of having drinks with these friends and sharing the hardships of trying to build a brand, or asking for their advice as I fleshed out my brainchild. My squad always cheered me on. They always encouraged me to go after my dreams.

A lot of the time I learned just by shutting up and paying attention. I was like a fly on the wall as Jessica Alba, whom I knew from my early salon days, started building The Honest Company. She recognized that there was a set of customers whose needs weren't being met, and she created a business around them. She saw the purchasing power of mothers who, until then, had largely been addressed by old white men at big corporations who couldn't relate to their experience. (My words, not hers.) She understood the value of speaking her customers' language and appealing to their intelligence *and* their style.

I had a similar experience with the Kardashian-Jenner family. It took way too long for people to give them the credit they deserved when it came to their business savvy. These women were approaching the female consumer in a whole new way, and maybe they were written off—as vain or flighty or who knows what—but that didn't stop them from building an empire. Appealing to smart female consumers was a commonality of so many of the successful women around me. Plus, I nabbed a front-row seat to Kris Jenner's genius and got to observe a true master as she flawlessly navigated licensing deals, collaborations, and business partnerships. I couldn't have learned any of that in business school.

Watching my friends and clients become entrepreneurs and turn their passions into profitable businesses has been an incredibly valuable and meaningful experience for me. And the best part of it all is the fact that this community of women is only interested in lifting one another up, sharing intel, and celebrating each other's success. My tribe of ladies inspired one another and encouraged one another and rooted for one another during every phase of our careers. Rather than feeling envious of someone else's achievements, we were proud—because we all felt invested in that person and her business. And each person's success inspired the rest of us to keep going.

Today I love nothing more than bragging about my girlfriends, who at this point are killing it across multiple industries. Honestly, I have goose bumps just writing this, because seeing my friends get rewarded with much-deserved success after witnessing them work their asses off and deal with people doubting them for years . . . it's everything. Moral of the story: success takes a village, and there's no better village to inspire success than a community of strong women.

YOUR BODY IS A WONDERLAND

Okay. Listen up. This one is important, and I know it might be an unexpected opinion to hear from someone who makes people look glam for a living. But. While it's awesome to feel pretty and fun to have great hair . . . there are more important things.

I know you know this. Intellectually, deep down, you are aware, obviously, that your physical appearance isn't your value. But I also know that we have all been raised in a world that tells us through TV, movies, and advertising that a woman's physical appearance is valued over, well, pretty much everything. We judge women for the color of their hair or the shape of their butt, we scoff if they're too skinny and make comments if they're too big. And, of course, this external judgment gets internalized pretty quickly, which means the most critical voice in our head is usually our own.

I am a woman who grew up in America, which means that I am a woman who has felt shitty about her looks. It took me a long time to feel comfortable in my skin, and as a teenager my negative self-talk was LOUD. Growing up as one of the only brown kids in a homogeneous Utah community, it was easy to get caught up in the typical standards of beauty, like weight and body shape, and I certainly believed that I would somehow be "better" if only I looked different or weighed less. I mean, I was a teenager in the mid-nineties, when "scary skinny" was all the rage. The Atkins diet was in full effect and, hello, I *had* to try it, it was my namesake. But, man, when I look back at my younger self now, at the girl who used to run on the treadmill for an hour a day and obsess over her diet and hate her hips, I want to shake her and say, "Just eat the bread at Arby's, everything's going to be fine!" I wish that girl could have known that one day she'd work out to gain energy rather than to lose weight, and that her career success would speak louder than any number on a scale.

Over the years, I've learned to go easier on myself. That's mostly a product of getting older, and the realization, cliché as it may be, that I should be grateful for everything my body allows me to do instead of beating it up for not looking a certain way. Now I think about my overall health instead of my carb intake.* Moving my body on a regular basis isn't about burning calories, it's about feeling strong, preventing disease, and releasing stress and anxiety.

But my improved body attitude has also come from being a hairstylist who has clients—both celebrities and regular ladies alike—who spend a lot of their time in the chair complaining about their bodies and fixating on their flaws. These are women of all shapes and sizes, and honestly, they all look great. It's heartbreaking to listen to them berate themselves, completely unforgiving of any supposed imperfections. And it reminds me that I have a responsibility, as the founder of a beauty line, to help redefine our standards of beauty. At OUAI, we've made a point of including every body type, every race, every different look in our ad campaigns, and that inclusivity is something I'm extremely proud of. When I was a kid, I hardly saw any women who looked like me in ad campaigns or on TV. The only brown entertainers I had to look up to were Paula Abdul and Sade. So I'm glad to be able to play a small part in addressing the representation problem. Not to mention the fact that it has made our advertisements so much more real and interesting and inviting.

It's ridiculous to expect that you're going to spend your whole life physically fit and looking "perfect" (and "perfect" is really just an arbitrary standard created by the patriarchy, anyway). Your attitude toward your body, like your weight, will go up and down over the years, but I encourage you to stop and think about how much precious

---

* *Basically, I stopped going to Taco Bell and switched to Chipotle because I want to live forever.*

time and energy you're wasting obsessing over your looks when you could be investing it in relationships, or creative pursuits, or, I don't know, watching the RBG documentary.

Maybe you're starting to wonder, right about now, how a celebrity hairstylist and creator of a hair- and body-care line can say that looks don't matter. But that's not entirely what I'm saying. Your looks matter if feeling fresh puts pep in your step and helps you feel empowered. But your kindness, your generosity, your sense of humor, your strength of character—those things matter more. They're what people will remember when you're gone. This is not to diminish the fun that goes into changing up your look, or the extra oomph that comes when you get a glimpse in the mirror and are totally feeling yourself. Dressing up is fun! Feeling like your best self, inside and out, is an instant pick-me-up. I understand that 100 percent. The problems arise when you change your look in order to please someone else or win approval of others rather than to shine a light on your best self. (Insert Lizzo song here.)

I am all about aesthetic and liking the way you look. There's so much power in feeling good about yourself, inside and out. And I want that to come from within, I really do. But I also realize that some days you just feel . . . icky . . . and no amount of internal pep-talking is going to change that. For those days, here's what I've learned: Tighten that ponytail. Dress for your body (not for the body you wish you had, or the body of a model/actress/athlete who has an entirely different shape than you, but the body you are lucky enough to call yours). Find the parts you love about yourself, practice saying nice things to your body every day, and you'll shake the pressures society puts on you to look a certain way.

LOVE AND MARRIAGE

Mike and I dated for five years before we even thought about getting married. Back then, my feed was an endless scroll of weddings and babies, and my personal life was an endless barrage of questions. All anyone wanted to know was when we were getting married, and when we eloped to Paris, the questions immediately became "when are you going to get pregnant?" It was frustrating to me then, and sometimes it still is, because I worked so hard to make a name for myself and build a career and suddenly all anyone wanted to talk to me about was marriage and kids. It felt like I had traveled back in time, back to the life in Utah I made such a point to get away from.

As you know, I never had any desire to get married. I didn't dream about my wedding dress, and when Mike actually *did* propose, I was borderline mad at him because he knew I wanted us to be like Goldie Hawn and Kurt Russell! I loved that he was showing up every day because he wanted to, not because he was legally required to do so. But the nice Jewish boy warmed the Grinch's cold heart, and today I find marriage really incredible—life gets harder as you get older, and there's something nice about waking up every morning with a good guy. I had to get to that place in my own time, though, no matter how many bridal gowns started clogging my feed years before I was ready. I didn't let Pinterest (or my mother) rush me.

I think part of the reason I delayed marriage for as long as I did was because I worried that getting married would set me back in my career. Mike and I made a pact early on to be supportive of each other's ambitions and tolerant of the demands on each other's schedules, but even with the most supportive partner in the world, it's a tricky-slash-impossible balance to pull off (more on that soon). We just do our best. We try to set limits on how long we're apart (though there have been times when we haven't seen each other for months—thank you, FaceTime!), we both go to bed early when one of us has a predawn call time in the morning, and we don't sweat it too much if the other one isn't able to attend a big work event. We try to share things we love about each other and focus less on the stuff that bugs us. When you don't have a ton of quality time together, I think that's really important. Growing up, I watched my grandma and grandpa Atkin have the most loving and special relationship, and I try every day to emulate that. I never heard either of them say a bad word about the other. They whistled together in the morning, and prayed together before bed. They were best friends and it was beautiful.

In the end, I got married because I knew this was a man who would support my dreams rather than try to stifle them. It wasn't about the pressure to be paired off, or any internal belief that having a husband would somehow make me whole. I've had so many clients, usually women, who value themselves according to what relationship they're in—as if they have nothing to offer until they've got someone by their side. Everyone deserves love, but the minute you believe you need a romantic relationship in order to feel good about yourself or to be a "success" in the larger context of life, you're in dangerous territory. If you decide to get married, please do it because you want to . . . never because you need to. Don't let outside pressure to live your life a certain way add to your ever-growing list of stressors.

THIS IS WHAT A FEMINIST MAN LOOKS LIKE

At this point in my life, I barely have any friends, male or female, who don't consider themselves feminists. Everybody's better off when women have more rights or when there's more gender equality in the home, and the men in my life understand this. Trust me when I say that the guys I know who are confident enough to support their breadwinning wives and help push their careers forward are doing *juuuuuussssst* fine. They have great lives, and if anyone judges the fact that their wives are the bigger earners . . . well, I assume they just laugh about that all the way to their Realtor's office.

I can't exactly speak for men, but from what I can see, at least in L.A., the old story line that a man needs to be the breadwinner in order to feel good about himself is becoming less predominant. As is the idea that men aren't attracted to women who are more successful than they are. It's a tired (and boring) old stereotype. In fact, in a lot of the successful heterosexual couples I know, the woman is the top earner. I know this isn't the case across America, but it's pretty awesome to witness the change starting. Strong men don't feel threatened by their wives' successes, and they certainly aren't embarrassed to call themselves feminists. When I listen to guys like America's favorite crooner, John Legend, publicly state that "all men should be feminists," it makes me feel so proud and so heartened. And I can say with total certainty that if it weren't for my supportive feminist husband, there is no way I would have been able to build my businesses. If I had an insecure partner who was resentful of my dedication to my job, it would have been game over. And if I was constantly worrying that he would be hurt or upset if I occasionally had to be at work instead of at home, I would have lost my career momentum long ago. Mike supports me, as I support him, and I don't have to worry about any sort of fragile male ego getting in the way. Everybody wins. Because there are always new goals to achieve and obstacles to overcome, for both of us, and I love that we support each other through that.

When it comes to gender equity, there's still a lot of work to be done. But I'm encouraged by the fact that an increasing number of men are coming to understand in a very real way that there is so much to be gained from having a variety of perspectives at the table. Colin, OUAI's CEO, often comments on how amazing it is to watch our team, built of mostly women, do such an incredible job of supporting each other but also understanding and supporting our customers. So I say the same thing to feminist men as I say to feminist women: Walk the walk. Bring your values into the workplace. Invest in women. Speak up for the women in your life who feel they don't have a voice or are afraid to use it. Question any anti-feminist conversations you hear amongst men. This shouldn't only be the responsibility of female founders or female CEOs. This is on all of us.

NEVERTHELESS, SHE PERSISTED

My own feminism has been informed by an interesting and unexpected combination of, first, being a girl raised in a religious community; second, being a hairstylist who helps women contend with their baggage around their physical appearance; and, finally, being a woman in business. I have more experience than I'd like in areas where women, and particularly Black women, have typically been oppressed or underrepresented, and I've seen the way that treatment manifests for them on the inside and out. Bearing witness to this has been, at times, pretty heartbreaking.

But there is good news. I feel so much hope for the next generation of women. Uh, look at Greta Thunberg, Yara Shahidi, Emma Gonzalez, Nadya Okamento, Malala Yousafzai, Jamie Margolin, Irsa Hirsi! In the years I've been behind the chair, so much has changed. The young women I meet or hear from today, whether they're my followers or up-and-coming stylists, are changing history. They are finding mentors and mentoring others. They are using their voice, in the workplace and in society. They are self-aware and knowledgeable about where change needs to happen. They are eager to share their stories. Never before have young people had so many tools to create change, and I find the promise of the next generation so inspiring and exciting. I may be sharing my advice for them—for YOU!—but I know it won't be long before you're the ones schooling me.

Shooting on set for Slip with my little rescue pup Roo—2019

My Beverly Hills courthouse wedding to Mike
Rosenthal, wearing a navy suit and Grandma Atkin's
brooch—2015

CHAPTER EIGHT
BALANCE IS BULLSHIT (BUT YOU CAN STILL TRY)

n 2017, about a year after OUAI launched, I boarded a plane bound for Paris, as I had for the past ten years. I was on my way to Fashion Week, where I was going to style clients for events and shows, but this time, instead of feeling excited and grateful, I was exhausted and stressed. I'd been working nonstop since starting the business, while still trying to keep up with Mane Addicts and my celebrity clients' demanding schedules and creating my social media content and doing meet-and-greets and photo shoots of my own. There were so many amazing things happening, and from the outside my life looked pretty great. And yet on the inside I was falling apart. I was only one person, with only twenty-four hours in the day. I had more responsibilities than I ever could have imagined, and it all happened far more quickly than I ever could have expected.

The reality was simple: I was in over my head. I was

becoming known for canceling meetings or rescheduling appointments at the last minute. Time management had always been a struggle—I try to fit too much into a day— but now, I realized, my workaholic nature was actually negatively affecting other people. I bit off more than I could chew because I didn't want to disappoint anyone, and yet that's exactly what I ended up doing, because I just couldn't manage it all. I was late for clients, late for meetings, late for dinners. Every single day I felt the stress that there wasn't enough time to get everything done. And I hadn't stolen a single moment in the previous twelve months to breathe or relax or reflect on how I might manage things better.

The second I sat down in Air France seat 5A, it all came raining down on me: the endless to-do lists, the looming deadlines, the fear of letting down the people who relied on me or the followers cheering me on every day. As the plane took off, I pulled my blanket over my head and cried. And cried and cried. All the emotions I'd been bottling up and ignoring because I didn't have time for them came pouring out. It was exhausting and cathartic and completely, 100 percent necessary.*

It didn't take long for the flight attendant to check on me. "I just need to cry," I told her. And so I came out from under my blanket, accepted a glass of pinot grigio, and watched a marathon of tearjerkers—movies like *The Notebook* and *Beaches*—because I wanted to let the well run dry. I'm not much of a crier—especially in public—but there I was.

---

* *Transatlantic flights are great for this kind of emotional release.*

There's a misconception that once you achieve your dreams or become the boss, you'll be able to delegate the hard work and take back your personal life. What happens instead—or at least what happened for me—is just the opposite. The more successful I became, the more pressure I felt, because more people were relying on me and more money was at stake. To this day, every time I take on a new project, I have that moment where I think: *What did I just do? How much more of myself did I just commit to something else?* I've seen the same thing play out with some of my clients. We all work so hard, but it's not like when we reach our goals our problems disappear. You are still you, with all the same baggage and personal needs, but maybe even less time to deal with them.

Obviously I'm not the first career-driven woman to deal with this issue. Today it seems like "balance" is the ultimate buzzword in regard to the work-life juggle, and while that kind of equilibrium is a worthy goal, achieving an even split among the many areas of your life is pretty much impossible. This goes for the career women *and* the stay-at-home moms who put pressure on themselves to do it all perfectly. I think the sooner we all accept the truth—and stop putting pressure on ourselves to achieve some unattainable Pinterest goal—the better chance we'll all have of creating a version of our lives that works for us.

THE PANIC BUTTON

While my in-flight breakdown forced me to face some hard facts, the truth is that my life fell out of

balance long before I launched OUAI. I take full responsibility for that, because rather than guarding my personal
time in the early days, I made a big show of proving that I
was all about working 24/7.* When I visited my parents for
the holidays in 2015, I sat my family down to warn them
that I'd probably be too busy to see them for a while. "I just
want to tell you guys that I'm going to be MIA for the next
few years," I said. "Things are about to get really crazy, so
you're going to need to forgive me in advance for being a
bad daughter and sister." They were all pretty taken aback,
but at the time I thought I was doing the right thing by
preparing them. And maybe I was, because I really didn't
come around much in those next few years—I actually
was working constantly, and I told myself it was okay to
shut myself off from family and friends. I thought I was
being responsible. In the movies, this is what successful
sacrifice looked like . . . loneliness. The good news is that
my family is wonderful and they love me unconditionally,
so rather than being annoyed or angry, they were super-
proud of me. Or maybe they were half annoyed and half
proud, but that was good enough for me. (And luckily, time
heals most wounds.)

When I look back at just how career-focused I was back
then, it's clear that some of my behaviors veered into the
obsessive category. There's a thin line between dedication
and addiction, and I'm not sure I always fell on the right
side of it. I've mentioned already that when my career first
started picking up and I was juggling a bunch of different
projects, I kept a spreadsheet of exactly how much money

---

* *My therapist says this is called "hiding in your work."*

I made every single day. When you grow up listening to your parents stress about finances, the fear of not having enough can embed itself into your psyche and become your downfall. I was so focused on the dollar that I was prioritizing it over my relationships or my health and even my happiness. Fortunately, I had the instinct to rein in that behavior early on, hire a business manager, and delegate the money obsession to someone else (stay tuned for details in Chapter Nine)—but the fixation on being busy and having more to do and saying yes to every project didn't subside. My work was my life, and gradually the passion I had for my craft morphed into a negative force that took over my world. I had everything I ever wanted but I wasn't able to come up for air. I started to exist in an almost constant state of panic—I couldn't even get rest in my sleep. Instead I dreamed about work, grinding my teeth at night and sleeping with my hands balled into such tight fists that I'd wake up wondering why my fingers were sore.

Despite all these red flags, I didn't realize just how unbalanced my life had become until December of 2018. The holidays are always stressful for me—for the usual holiday season reasons, but also because my clients are usually super-busy with projects and events before the end of the year, which means my schedule gets extra-crazy. I've always taken a lot of pride in being able to handle and delegate an ambitious workload, but that year I was also wrapping up our biggest OUAI campaign to date, and Mike and I had just rescued a dog, Roo, and bought a house. We were trying to sell the house we lived in, and I was coming off the reveal of my first luggage collection. The previous month, in a span of one week, I'd flown from L.A. to Dubai to NYC to Las Vegas and back to L.A., doing twenty-one cuts a day on the days I was working in the salon. (For those working out the math at home, I do the haircuts in thirty minutes, my assistants do the styling afterward.) Plus, OUAI had just announced that we took on a new investor, which for me felt a lot like telling my dad I got a credit card when I was nineteen. Scary and intimidating. Needless to say, I was feeling overwhelmed.

One night, just before bed, I mentioned to Mike that I thought I had heartburn. I figured I ate something weird, though I wasn't sure what that was. It felt like an elephant was sitting on my chest, making it hard to breathe, and my heart wanted to jump outside of my body. It was scary, but I tried to ignore it and eventually I fell asleep. An hour later I woke up to go to the bathroom. I was covered in sweat, and the minute I stood up I felt the room spin and then it went black. I had never fainted in my life, but I hit the ground with such a loud thud that it woke up Mike.

At the hospital, after a few blood tests and an IV, the doctors told me I was severely dehydrated and diagnosed me with a panic attack. (Drinking more water had been on my goals list for about three years.) Until that moment, I'd been the kind of person who rolled her eyes at the mention of these sorts of episodes. *So dramatic,* I once thought. But as soon as I got a better understanding of what had happened to me, I realized that I'd been having mini–panic attacks for a while, whenever I got on a plane. And I'm not just talking about crying-under-a-blanket-during-takeoff moments, but the cabin fever of "I'm stuck on this plane for fourteen hours and I have so much to do and can't handle being trapped in here." I had been taking nearly a hundred flights a year and a few Ambien here and there for at least five years. Still, the straight-up passing out in my hallway was the wake-up call I needed. That's when I started to reevaluate my schedule and my priorities, and when I finally accepted that I needed to take better care of myself. I started exercising again, I replaced Diet Coke with iced tea, and, most importantly, I spent time with our new dog. Roo is my baby. She's registered as an emotional support animal, and there is no question that she takes care of me as much as I take care of her.

My panic attack was my body's way of telling me that my lifestyle wasn't working. The distribution of my time and energy was totally out of whack, and I had no choice but to make a change. Sometimes the scariest moments are really a blessing in disguise.

TAKE BACK YOUR WEEKEND

One of my first post–panic attack resolutions was to start taking weekends off. This shouldn't be all that revolutionary, since most people work Monday through Friday, and yet I'm pretty sure I worked every single Saturday from 2007 to 2017. I'm serious. Saturdays are the busiest days at any salon. As a hairstylist, you want to be there, because you could easily do the same amount of business on a Saturday that you might on two weekdays combined. I was also the kind of person who put self-care second to working or helping other people, so my default was to always say yes to projects and take on the world and worry later about the logistics of managing it all. The problem with this approach is that you give yourself no time to recharge. By working all weekend every weekend, you give up the days that you would otherwise use to nurture relationships, or take care of your health, or—gasp!—just relax and do nothing. (On the plus side, I saved a lot of money, since I never had time to go shopping or out to lunch. But overall? Two stars. Would not recommend.) Mike would watch me slump onto the couch at the end of a long week, or listen to me bitch about my schedule, and he got understandably tired of my negativity. "Most people have a weekend," I remember him telling me. "Your Saturday-night meltdowns are unsustainable." It wasn't until he got sick and tired of me being sick and tired that I made the deliberate decision to take weekends off entirely.

This was not an easy change to make. I don't want to minimize the difficulty of slowing down when you're someone who has spent years going at top speed. The change of pace can feel really uncomfortable at first, and that was definitely true in my case because I relied on my work for validation. It was an odd sensation to have such freedom. Instead of having every hour—and I mean, to the minute—scheduled for some kind of work, I could make the choice to go for a walk or sit in the sun or watch TV or do . . . anything. Or nothing. I had forgotten what that was like, and at first I didn't know what I wanted to do. I felt like I should use the newfound time productively—if I wasn't going to work, shouldn't I catch up on emails or finally sort through the Pinterest boards I'd been meaning to organize? But then I remembered that those tasks counted as work, too, even if I wasn't actually doing hair. I also fell into the trap of second-guessing myself and my choices after seeing the action on Instagram. I would take a Saturday off, then I'd see a hairdresser on set doing the job that I'd turned down, and immediately feel guilty for not giving 100 percent. Even though I'd reached a point in my career where I could afford to say no to some job offers, it was hard to shake the hustler mindset that my livelihood relied on booking the next gig. I know it sounds twisted, but I felt like every time I turned down a job I was signaling to the Universe that I was ungrateful for the opportunities coming my way.

Still, I was committed to taking Saturdays and Sundays off, and after a couple months, I had a pretty major realization: nothing suffered. I didn't lose out on anything. For so long, I'd had this idea that if I slowed down for even a day, the train would stop running or the offers would stop coming in or my income would get slashed. But no. My businesses continued to thrive, my teams stayed busy, my services were still in demand, my clients kept calling. If anything, my work improved, and I found myself saying I *get* to go to work rather than I *have* to go to work. Slowing down, I learned, doesn't have to mean losing business. No matter your job, if you earn the loyalty of clients or the trust of colleagues, the opportunities will still be there on Monday.

Another reason I had avoided taking weekends off, or having downtime in general, was that I feared being relaxed would make it harder to ramp back up to workaholic mode. I didn't want to take the holidays off at the end of the year or go on vacations with my husband because I was worried about slowing down. I figured it would be like the few times I've tried giving up carbs—everything's going great until you have that bite of a dinner roll and suddenly you're knee-deep in a basket of Little Caesars Crazy Bread. The minute I got a taste of what time off felt like, I worried there would be no coming back from it. But the opposite happened. I took the weekend, or even sometimes a vacation, and by the time Monday rolled around I was refreshed and ready to go and even excited to dive back in. Shocking. It was a huge benefit to my team, who needed me to be at my best. It's not particularly helpful to have a boss who's running at half capacity during meetings because she's exhausted and burned-out and complaining under her breath. If you have a boss who isn't happy, it's contagious. Not to mention the fact that whenever I was working, my team was working beside me . . . meaning that their weekends were also cut short. A business with happy and engaged employees is always going to be more productive, and everyone is happier when they can sleep in on Saturday.

These days, I'm addicted to having my weekend. I needed to learn the art of recharging, but now that I have, I see the benefits so clearly. I laugh again. I smile more. I started having my friends and their families over. I got to spend time with my young nieces and nephews. Our house started to feel like a home. Taking a break from checking my phone or answering emails for two full days gave me life. I'd never had that ability to disconnect from the work before, and it feels like a real achievement. You have to be able to celebrate your wins, and the best takeaway from working my ass off for all those years is that I don't have to anymore.

In reality, I probably could have worked less, and relaxed more, long before this. In 2017, I didn't work out for the entire year because I didn't have the energy and I felt so weak.

I also didn't go to the doctor for about a decade, because hairstylists don't get health insurance and I couldn't imagine actually investing in my health. I cheated myself out of having a life and taking care of myself, and I regret it.

Although weekends have become sacred, there are still a few stretches a year where I might go on a two- or three-week run with no day off, and when that happens I feel myself start to get resentful. The thing I love most about the weekend other than, well, the weekend, is that knowing it's coming gets me through the busy periods. Even during my most recent two-week stretch, I was able to remind myself toward the end that "I just need to get through today." It makes the all-work-no-play periods easier to bear. I've also learned that I don't have to suffer in silence, so now I'm better about communicating with my team and my therapist when I'm drowning and need help.

Take it from me: the people who manage their growing careers best are those who have valued and prioritized self-care throughout the journey, so start now. Learn from my mistakes, so you don't find yourself releasing your tears into a Barefoot Dreams blanket on the plane. You'll thank me one day.[*]

MAKE TIME FOR ME-TIME

Even after I balanced my schedule in terms of workdays and weekends—or at least created a schedule that

---

[*] *Also, Flying Pro Tip: Never take a sleeping pill until the plane is actually in the air.*

resembled something closer to balance—I noticed that I still rarely had time alone. I wanted to use my weekends to connect with Mike, since workdays were so crazy, or to see all the friends I'd been missing for a decade. I didn't do nearly as well at carving out time for just myself, even though I'm someone who gets a rush of energy from having quiet moments alone. Today, I try hard to focus on fitting that in, if not daily, then at least weekly. I love manicures and massages because they combine luxurious pampering with time to be alone with your thoughts and clear your head. Exercise, too—less luxurious, but essential in the head-clearing category. And I schedule ninety-minute blocks of alone time into my calendar, for reading, meditating, writing, napping, or any combination of those things.

I also try to designate one night a week to get nine hours of sleep, and I've stopped watching TV, sending emails, or scrolling social when I should be in bed. Everyone's different, but I'm one of those people who needs a lot of sleep. More than the seven to eight hours that doctors recommend, that's for sure. In my natural state I could probably sleep for ten or eleven hours a night, but during the week I get more like six and a half to seven. For me, sleep changes everything. I can be upset or stressed or annoyed, but if I get enough sleep, I wake up with the same attitude that my dog has every morning. *OMG, I'm alive! Let's go! Let's do something!*

For many of us, downtime is such a rarity that when we have it, figuring out how to use it becomes a challenge in itself. If you're not sure what to do with your time, might I suggest discovering a hobby? Or how about doing nothing?

Just enjoying the quiet? There's this myth that we need to be productive at all times, that if you have time to relax it means you're lazy or not doing enough, and that's total B.S. Let's squash this Burnout Generation stereotype. Please, don't avoid having downtime, and don't feel guilty for basking in those free moments. Also, downtime doesn't mean scrolling through social media! We spend so much time looking down—at our computers or our desks or our phones. Try to see what happens when you change your perspective. Look up. Taking advantage of leisure time is not a sign that you have nothing "more important" to do; it's a sign that you value your health and your sanity and you're comfortable with your own thoughts.

PUT DOWN THE PHONE

Have you ever thought about how many hours a day you spend staring at a screen? Do you feel naked when you don't have your phone in your hand? Do you check your notifications before getting out of bed in the morning?

Our society has a phone addiction. I'm not telling you anything you don't already know, but it's pretty wild when you stop to think about it. Until recently, anytime I got together with friends, the first thing we did was whip out our phones to document the moment. Then there was all the time we spent checking and answering texts and emails and Stories and DMs and tweets—the sense of urgency created by immediate access is completely toxic.

For a long time I was probably more guilty than most of this screen addiction. That is, until I went on a weeklong mental health retreat where I was forced to surrender my phone. There are all types of these retreats all over the world. The one I went to was called the Hoffman Process. And it was a . . . whole . . . week . . . unplugged. It seemed legitimately impossible at first, and really f'ing scary, but in the end it was life-changing. Once I let go of the overwhelming urge to check my notifications every few seconds, the nervousness and stress of being on call dissipated, and I realized that I'd been walking around constantly on guard. *What's that text? What about that email? OMG a notification! Is that my WhatsApp? Gotta check my DMs and do my Insta Story and see if my captions are ready.* Stepping out of that fray for even just a moment, I was struck by a sense of contentedness I hadn't felt in a DECADE. It was so . . . pleasant. And calm. I lived the first twenty years of my life without being tethered to a phone, but I'd completely forgotten what that felt like. Once I returned from the retreat, I was desperate not to lose that feeling, and I've since been making a concerted effort to separate myself from my phone whenever possible.

Of course, even when you've gotten over the psychological difficulty of unplugging, and by that I mean the FOMO and the guilt of not responding immediately to every communication, there are some real logistical complications of putting down the phone. First, there's the simple fact that we rely on our phones for *everything*—I've had to order an old-fashioned battery-operated alarm clock just so I can go to sleep without my phone sitting inches away from my head. You might have to order your lunch at an actual restaurant instead of on an app. Or purchase an item in a store instead of with a swipe.

There's also the reality that even if you've decided to take a break from your device, the rest of the world is still connected to theirs. Recently I was on set for a job and I didn't want to waste my lunch hour staring at a screen. But as soon as we broke for lunch, every single person immediately whipped out their phone. I had nobody to talk to, because everyone else was so busy scrolling their feeds. I ended up going for a walk along the ocean by myself and sitting down for a few moments to meditate, and I felt great afterward. It was so crazy to me that we were literally steps from the beach yet everyone passed their lunch hour inside, staring at a screen. I understand that the level of technology access we've become accustomed to is a real blessing, but whatever happened to eye contact? To being interested in other human beings and making conversation? It really feels like we've stopped living our own lives to watch everyone else's.

Once I decided to scale back my screen use, I had to tell my friends and colleagues that I wasn't going to be staring at my phone all the time, so if they really needed me they were going to have to . . . drum roll . . . make a phone call. It's been a good approach for a number of reasons. First, it forces me to have actual real-life conversations, which is almost always more efficient than prolonged text exchanges. Plus, it forces people to decide if the issue they want to discuss is urgent enough to warrant a phone call. Most people would rather avoid talking live, which means they usually think twice before calling. The way I see it, if someone really needs me, they'll pick up the phone, but if my input isn't essential, I find that people are often more inclined to just handle it themselves. Texting, on the other hand, is so easy that my team sometimes reaches out before even considering if they can solve the problem on their own. I'm not discouraging calls—I love hearing my team members' voices—but sometimes we're so quick to text someone else for their input that we create inefficiencies and lose out on valuable opportunities to learn.

These days I like to think of myself as a reformed texter. Like everyone else, I grew so accustomed to text and email and DM that, for a long time, the idea of actually *talking* to someone made me cringe. It got to a point where I needed practice talking with people and seeing them in real life and hugging them (you don't get a serotonin hit through texting) and looking them in the eyes rather than sitting alone with my neck down staring at a screen. That's how dire it's gotten for many of us: we actually need to practice talking with friends. Now I love picking up the phone and calling someone. I've been trying to call one random friend a day, just to engage in the underrated art of old-fashioned conversation.

I should add that my body has told me in many different ways that my phone addiction was hurting me. There was the panic attack and the plane-crying episode, but then in June 2019 I was diagnosed with a herniated disc that resulted in months of neck and back pain (Tech Neck is a real thing), a neck brace, bed rest, and ten months of physical therapy. My body was yelling, *Help! Help! I need attention!* But it took barely being able to turn my head for me to actually listen.

Not long ago, Mike and I hosted a dinner party for eight couples—some of them influencers you probably follow, plus their significant others. At the start of the evening, we welcomed our guests at the door with a bag to drop their phones into. I wanted everyone to really be present. They thought we were crazy at first—these are people who post a video the moment they arrive anywhere, because their businesses are built on sharing their lives—but we ended up having a truly epic game night, and at the end of the evening no one even wanted their phones back. It was so freeing. Nobody felt compelled to document every moment of the night or had to worry about what they looked like in someone else's post. I highly recommend trying a "phone-free" dinner with friends or your partner—you'll be surprised at how much more relaxed everyone feels, and I bet you'll connect on a deeper level.

Sometimes it feels like *The Walking Dead* out there, with everyone looking at their phones 24/7, but it doesn't have to be that way. "Pics or it didn't happen" isn't a real thing. Remember that. It happened, you just need to experience it when it does.

YOU CAN'T DO IT ALONE

There is no doubt in my mind that I'd still be working 110 percent of the time if I hadn't eventually learned to embrace asking for help. No single person can do everything—and they certainly can't do everything at once. If I hadn't been willing to call in reinforcements to help me manage my workload, I never would have been able to take back my weekends or make time for my marriage or disappear for a week to go to a much-needed unplugged therapy retreat.

•

One of the things that makes me feel luckiest is the fact that I'm surrounded by a kick-ass team. When I realized I had to figure out a better system for managing my career because I was getting a lot of asks and couldn't be in multiple places at once (believe me, I tried), my team stepped up. By that point I'd put a lot of time and effort into teaching them, because I wanted them to have the tools they needed to continually improve. It can be hard to nurture your own creativity and ambition while also giving attention to the people working around you, but I wouldn't have seen any of my own success if I hadn't had mentors who invested their time and energy and knowledge in me, and I always wanted to do the same once I had a team of my own.

We nicknamed the core group the Jen Atkin Army, and it was a win for everyone. I got a break, they got to fly solo, and my clients got the treatment they'd learned to expect from assistant stylists they'd already met and had trusted for years. When I first made the change, I was nervous that my clients would feel abandoned. But it wasn't like I fell off the face of the earth. In fact, they were happy for me—they knew how hard I'd been pushing myself, and they could feel that my energy had been getting more intense. Plus, if anyone could relate, it was my clients. These women were working just as hard if not harder than I was. And it was so great to see my assistants rise to the occasion. I remember when I first sent Justine to style Khloé Kardashian on her own because I was suddenly occupied with responsibilities at OUAI. The old thinking in my industry is that you would never do something like that for fear of losing a valuable client, but to me it was a perfect solution—everyone was taken care of and comfortable, Justine got to take on a big job, and it was clear that my time training her was well spent.

When I decided I wanted to start taking weekends off, I had to have an honest conversation with my team and my agents and face my biggest fear: admitting defeat. That's what it felt like at first, like I'd been beaten down by the work, or that I couldn't hack it anymore. We were on a con ference call, and when the words came out all I could say was, "I'm human, and I'm really exhausted." I explained that I had finally gotten everything I'd dreamed of, but that I was a shell of myself and, as a result, my work wasn't as good as it could be. I wasn't as creative in meetings, and I wasn't thinking as clearly. I guess I expected some push-back, but I got none. It was as if they'd been waiting for me to come to this conclusion, and they were ready to jump in and do what they could to help. Nobody was disappointed like I imagined they'd be. They were beyond supportive, and I'm not sure I would have been able to do it if they hadn't been.

It's natural, in this world that values self-sufficiency and hustle, to feel that you should shoulder all your work alone. Maybe you think you should be able to handle whatever life throws at you, or that you don't want to bother anyone by asking for their help. Or maybe you just think every-thing would get done faster or better if you did it yourself, or that it would take longer to train someone else than it would for you to just handle the work on your own. But none of us works alone. No one finds success without sup-port behind them. And you will not find any version of balance in your life if you don't let people you trust take things off your plate. Repeat after me: asking for help is OKAY!

YOU'LL GROW OUT OF IT

Balance looks different depending on who you are, or even where you are in your life. Admittedly, it has looked dramatically different for me through the years—the work and life goals of twenty-year-old Jen were very different from the forty-year-old version. My twenties were about making my mark on the world and getting my name out there, which meant saying yes to work *and* fun. I have no regrets, but balance back then meant going out and not sleeping and still being able to go to work and be alert. I was seriously focused on balancing my budget, because I had no money. In my early twenties, being social was more important to me than being a hard worker—I was partying *a lot*—and I probably could have tipped the scales a bit more toward the work side of things.

It was in my late twenties that things started to shift. I saw my friends less and let work take over. That's when I started making money, which brought my attention to the budget-balancing I mentioned. Balance meant saving that money rather than spending lavishly, which I didn't always succeed at. I often felt like I needed expensive things I couldn't afford to feel good about myself. I also struggled, as so many twentysomethings do, with what I thought my body *should* look like versus what it actually did look like. Remember that I spent the first half of that decade watching the skinny women on *Friends* and *Ally McBeal*. Ugh, we are so hard on ourselves in our twenties!

Balance in your thirties is different. The partying till dawn is no longer really a concern, because you can't drink or stay out the same way anymore . . . you feel it too hard the next day. The definition of fun changes—it looks more like a dinner party than going out to the club. You might be married with kids, or deep in career mode, or those things might be just around the corner, so you're trying to balance responsibility and a social life. That sometimes means weeding out the friends from your twenties who aren't a great influence on you anymore, or who aren't maturing at the same rate. Hopefully by your thirties you don't have time or energy to obsess about being thick or thin or looking a certain way, because you've got more pressing concerns about your body—is it healthy, can it run a marathon, can it carry a baby if that's what you want, that sort of thing. And there's a renewed focus on mental well-being versus just the physical. When I was thirty-eight, I decided to give up drinking altogether, because I realized that it made me feel crappy the next morning, and that I'd rather face whatever difficult feelings I was having head-on than try to drown them in wine. I'm old enough to realize that I'd rather feel good when I wake up than have another glass of sauvignon blanc just because I'm trying to be "fun."* Also, my executive assistant, Nicole, after hearing me complain for the 200th time about having low energy,

---

* *Even if it means 1.5 million people asking me if I'm pregnant because I stopped drinking. Grrr.*

said something that really hit home for me: "Drinking is essentially stealing tomorrow's happiness." Bingo.

The pressure is on, in your thirties, to start thinking about becoming financially prepared for the future, so balancing immediate needs with long-term ones becomes a more urgent focus. And this is when a career more typically starts to take off, so really thinking through what your work-life distribution looks like, or what you want it to look like, becomes necessary. You also, hopefully, start to think more about other people and the world around you.

And in your forties . . . well, I'm just starting out. What I can already tell is that there's a renewed respect for personal time and its importance to overall well-being. My clients tell me that in your forties, as a woman, you get a newfound appreciation for your body and hit a sexual peak. TBD, but I'm preparing Mike for anything and everything.

My hope for my forties is that I get more time for self-awareness and more time with our family. I want to show up more for the causes that need my attention. I want to volunteer more and use my platform to help make positive changes in neighborhoods that need it. I want to be more present across the board—present with Mike, present with the village that may help us raise our babies one day, present with the businesses and teams that work around me, and present with my family and friends and dogs. That right there sounds like a full day every day. And more alone time! I expect my next decade will be less of a "how do I balance work and play" and more of a "how do I distribute my attention between the many people, causes, and teams that need me" kind of quest.

ON BALANCING AMBITION AND LIFE CHOICES

never really wanted kids. Being a mother was never a priority for me, and that truth became even louder over time, as my clients who had kids divulged the hardest, grossest, scariest parts of childbirth. I could see that they were all really going through it, hormonally, because they would come into the salon and ask me to chop their hair off or cut bangs—textbook reactions to the turmoil brought on by a major life event. (Ask any hairstylist: when a client sits in the chair and says, "Take it all off!," it's a red flag. That doesn't mean we won't do it, of course, but it's rarely about the hair.) For many of my new mama clients, changing up their hair was a way to shift the focus away from their bodies, because they weren't feeling good in their own skin. A number of my clients experienced postpartum depression. It became increasingly clear to me that pregnancy and childbirth weren't for me. Raising kids wasn't conducive to my lifestyle, and I was too focused on my career to interrupt it for a family.

That said, I, like most women, started fielding baby questions around age thirty. Plenty of my friends were starting to have families, or at least considering the logistics of how they'd fit kids into their lives, but I never bothered with family planning, since I had no family plans. My biological clock never showed up.

That is, until I met Mike. It didn't take long, once we started dating, for me to see what an amazing father he would be. And he was always honest with me about the fact that he wanted kids—I, in turn, was honest with him that

I never felt the longing that so many women talked about. I didn't yearn to be a mother. There was no way I could do everything back then—broaden my career and build a business and start a family—and certainly not all at once, and I told Mike as much. By that point I also knew my limitations when it came to my own physical wellness. I'm fragile regarding body stuff. I had avoided going to doctors for about ten years not only because I didn't have health insurance, but also because I hate getting poked and prodded. Still, because I knew how important kids were to Mike, and because being with him made me wonder if eventually I *would* want kids, I decided to take matters into my own hands. I was thirty-five, and I still wasn't ready for kids, but I also knew that my body's biology was on a different timeline, and if, in my forties, I suddenly *was* ready, it could be too late.

So, a year after Mike and I got married, we decided to freeze embryos. For a long time, discussions about fertility were so hush-hush that I didn't even know there were ways to delay child-rearing. I thought it was a now-or-never kind of thing. But a few of my clients had gone through fertility treatments, so I decided to visit Dr. Andy Huang, a highly recommended reproductive endocrinologist, who talked to me about my options and reassured me that I could focus on my career now while still entertaining the idea of starting a family later. He presented two options: I could freeze my eggs, meaning I'd preserve eggs to be fertilized later, or I could freeze embryos, which meant fertilizing the egg with sperm now and saving the resulting embryos for the future when I was ready to have a baby. I took the embryo route, and I felt incredibly lucky, because I didn't have to choose between being a successful career woman and being a mother, if that became something I wanted. Freezing eggs or embryos can be prohibitively expensive, and sadly many insurance plans don't cover these procedures, so I realized how privileged I was to have the option. But I hope that changes, because the day I walked out of Dr. Huang's office with five embryos on ice, I felt like the weight of the world had been lifted off my shoulders.

It's a shame that we don't more openly discuss the options available to women who, for any number of reasons, might want or need to delay starting a family. My hope is that the more normalized it becomes, the more accessible it will become. Freezing my embryos gave me the power to dictate my own future. I could be in charge of my career, and my personal life, and the timing of it all. Balancing ambition with life choices is the hardest balance there is, and I find myself recommending embryo- or egg-freezing to girlfriends all the time—whether they want to have a family with a partner but haven't yet met the right person, or want to have kids but just not yet, or aren't sure what they want but don't want their biological clock making the call for them.

I shared my decision on Instagram, and posted from my doctor appointments, because it felt important to help erase the stigma and create a dialogue around family planning. The moment I did so, I can't tell you how many women came out of the woodwork to share that they'd done the same. I couldn't believe that this was all happening behind closed doors, and that some of my closest friends felt so much shame that they'd kept this very major life decision a secret. There's absolutely no reason that these conversations should be taboo, but the only way to change that is to share. I want people to know that egg-freezing is an option, because if you're someone who doesn't know if she wants kids, watching all your friends post pics of their growing families can be super-stressful. And if you're someone who wants kids but doesn't yet have them, looking at those same pics can be devastating.

Of course, I would be remiss if I didn't add that there's another amazing way to create a family on your own timeline, and that's adoption or fostering. I know people who have spent an incredible amount of money on IVF—going through multiple rounds and suffering the physical and emotional toll that takes—and I cannot stress enough that I would not be writing this book today if not for the opportunities given to me by my adoptive parents and my birth mother. I understand that adoption isn't the right choice for every family, but I think all the time about how lucky I am that my parents adopted me. Sometimes the only thing that separates us from people in really challenging situations is where we were born. My life could have turned out very differently if my birth mother hadn't made the choice she did. Obviously there's no way to know what would have happened if I hadn't been adopted, but there are no words to describe just how blessed I feel to have been given my family, and this life I've been lucky enough to have lived.

We can talk about self-image and self-confidence all day long, but being able to choose if and when to have a baby is, in my mind, an essential right that can dictate how a woman feels about herself and her life, maybe for her entire life. Mike and I were under tremendous pressure in the first few years of our marriage to have kids—the questions were *constant*—but I felt empowered to say, "We're just not ready." And he was completely supportive. It's not lost on me that so many girls and women worldwide don't have that freedom. When you're an ambitious career woman living in a society like ours, it's easy to get caught up in the girlbossiness of it all, cursing the fact that you are being forced to choose between having a family and having a career, but I try never to forget that at least I'm able to make the choice for myself. Not all women around the world are so lucky. Which reminds me: I send so much love to those who have struggled with the pain of infertility, miscarriage, or the death of a child. The psychological distress that women go through in a lifetime is overwhelming.

As I write this, I still don't have children. But I have a career that I gave my entire life to in my thirties, so that I could feel confident about scaling back in my forties without hurting the business. I have five embryos in a Los Angeles freezer. Mike and I are considering surrogacy, because my concerns about carrying a baby at my age are still real and still valid. But my choice is just that. My choice. I'm not here to say that what I did is for everyone or that it's the "right" way to plan a family. I have plenty of friends who decided to have kids while building their careers, and they figure it out as they go. They have amazing nannies or grandparents who help when they have to be away for work. It's not either-or, career or kids, but I knew myself well enough to know that, at least for a while, I would struggle to split my attention between a baby and a business (which is its own sort of baby) and do both jobs well. I'm starting to shift my mindset, but plenty of women who don't want kids in their twenties and thirties end up never wanting to have kids, and that is PERFECTLY OKAY, too! It's important to know who you are and what you want and not succumb to societal pressure, and I applaud the people who don't want kids and instead open their homes to rescued animals or invest their love in another way.

At the end of the day, you can only live your life the way it works for you. All I hope is that you will know that you don't have to give up your ambition because you want a family, and you don't have to give up having a family because you are ambitious. There are so many ways to navigate that balance. It's not always easy, but it's doable.

THE MAGIC WORDS: ROUTINE AND STABILITY

I have a job where no two days are alike. Bookings and meetings pop up at the very last minute. I might be in four different countries in one week. For a long time I lived in a constant state of jet lag, which can start to wear on your soul after a while. I had to laugh at the delight in my therapist's voice when I told him I was craving routine and stability. "Those are two words I never thought I'd hear from you," he told me.

These days I value predictability in my days above all else. Repetition might sound boring compared to jet-setting, but there is a lot to be said for the comfort of knowing what to expect when you wake up in the morning. Routine is the calm in the storm. On a particularly busy day, I might have a meet-and-greet, store visit, or meetings for OUAI in addition to all my usual work, which means I'll be talking to often hundreds of new people, and doing my best to connect with each of them. Some days I land, jet-lagged, in a foreign country, and the client wants to take me to dinner, which is so incredibly kind except I can barely keep my eyes open, and if I go out to dinner I know I'll wake up to a flood of emails because I didn't get around to answering them the night before. On days like that, I relish politely declining the unexpected fancy evening out and sticking to one routine, like going for a walk or meditating or doing a quick workout, and then getting those emails answered so I can relax and get a good night's sleep. Doing so reminds me that I am still in control. That my life hasn't entirely gotten away from me. That no matter what is going on with work, there are a few moments of my day where I don't have to go with the flow.

I should be clear that I'm still a work in progress when it comes to establishing order in my day, but I've learned that developing routines can be really simple—whatever makes you feel grounded and good counts. If I'm not traveling for work, I've started keeping a habit tracker and I try to follow my new home routine:

6:45	Wake up, no snooze, no phone
7-7:15	Feed and take out the dogs
7:15-7:30	Coffee, hot water with lemon
7:30-8	Work on gratitude list and habit tracker

8-9	Work out
9-9:15	Meditate
9:15-9:45	Eat breakfast, check texts
9:45-10:45	Shower, get dressed, do hair and makeup
10:45-1:30	Check phone, do Zooms and phone calls, work on scheduling, respond to emails
1:30-2	Lunch
2-5	IG Lives, content production, film social videos
5-7	Personal calls, walk dogs, texts
7-7:30	Dinner
7:30	Watch TV, read, play games
10:30	Get ready for bed
10:45	Sleep

I try to get a massage once a week. Mike and I have talked about doing Shabbat dinners, which would probably be a beautiful routine if we could get it together. (Like I said, work in progress.) None of these routines are earth-shattering or even particularly impressive, but just having some reliability in my life has created a lot of calm and comfort.

If and when we do have kids, I know that so many of these routines will go out the window, so I really try to soak it up while I can. And hopefully if that happens we'll develop new traditions.

Like I said, my therapist is proud.

THE BEAUTY OF COMPARTMENTALIZING

My very best advice for leaving work at work and home at home is to learn how to compartmentalize. Let's say you had a major setback with a project, or your boss called you out on a mistake. On a day like that, it's so easy to leave the office and take that stress home with you, where it seeps out onto the people around you. Similarly, if you spent the morning bickering with a roommate or partner, it's hard to head into the office with smile on your face and your usual can-do attitude. But when you train your brain to compartmentalize, at least as much as is reasonable, it's a lot easier to get through the day and do your best.

I had to hone my ability to compartmentalize as soon as I started taking on my own clients. I feel incredibly lucky that folks from all walks of life have entrusted me not only with their hair but with their innermost thoughts and their frustrations and fears, but—real talk—it can be a lot for one person to take on. I can't even imagine what it's like to be an actual therapist, because even for a pseudo-therapist like me it can be really draining.

I know this isn't unique to my job. Anyone who has to serve a client or report to a boss or collaborate with coworkers has likely had to absorb someone else's shitty mood. But we should take care not to let that energy, especially the negative energy, affect us too deeply. When I was starting out, I would come home from a *looooong* day of work and pass out on the couch. I was exhausted—physically, sure, but really it was a mental and emotional fatigue. I had spent the last twelve to fifteen hours acting as a sponge, listening to the good and bad things that were happening in my clients' days—maybe they had lost a job or a loved one, or they were going through a breakup or getting a promotion. I was constantly hearing the intimate details of their personal and professional lives, and a lot of times I was giving them advice. But the stress of that responsibility started to weigh on me. I was starting to bear other people's burdens, worrying about my clients around the clock, even when I wasn't at work. It's hard to not be affected by someone whose husband is cheating or who just lost a parent or had a big private story break in the *Daily Mail.* It was no one's fault, it's just that when people get their hair done, they sit back in the chair and unload all their baggage, and then move on with their day a little bit lighter. But when you're standing *behind* the chair, the hours upon hours of intense energy can really weigh you down. You have to learn how not to take on other people's stuff, and that's a constant challenge.

For a while, I wasn't especially good at this. I fully absorbed the energy that was coming at me, and it would really run me down. Anyone remember during quarantine when home became your gym, restaurant, spa, school, *and* office? We couldn't escape family, and parents became schoolteachers while trying to keep up with work Zooms? It was beyond hard for many of us to try to compartmentalize. I joked it shouldn't be called "work from home" but "live at work"! These days, I try to be more like a Teflon pan than a sponge. Instead of soaking up all that energy, I listen and engage and try to help but I don't let it stick.

The walk that Mike and I take with the dogs each evening has become a great buffer for me between work and home. We use the time to talk about our days and to get it all out, and then we let it go so we can enter our home with clear minds. Being outside also helps us transition out of the work headspace, because we'll stop to admire a tree or watch a sunset, and it's such a lovely reminder that the world is bigger than our jobs. Of course, we'll still catch each other here and there. We're far from perfect. But we try to (gently) call each other out when the stress of the workday creeps into our time together.

It's so L.A., I know, but meditating at least once in the morning has helped me a lot in terms of becoming more present and shutting out the noise.* I also try to give my brain distractions from stress and worry by listening to music and podcasts. I never want to arrive at a job feeling distracted and unengaged, so if I have a long drive from one job to another, I'll listen to a favorite podcast or blast some happy music to help clear my mind. I literally have a "Happy Songs" playlist, and yes, I sing along to it out loud. A little Lauryn Hill or Backstreet Boys will make any problem feel more manageable.

PERFECTLY IMPERFECT

No matter what your ideal balance looks like, it's important to remember that you will never be able to split your life perfectly between family and work and friends and self-care and all the many things you want to

---

* *I can't believe I've become one of those annoying advocates for meditation.*

devote your precious time to. You know what they say: you can have it all, but you can't have it all at the same time. Never let social media and the hustle porn fool you into believing otherwise.

Even when you make every intentional effort to divvy up your time wisely, each day will look different, and more often than not things won't go according to plan. You'll expect to have a quiet day of email catch-up and instead you'll get pulled into a work fire drill. You'll carve out time for a workout only to wake up with a stomach bug. The only way to survive the chaos with a smile on your face is to roll with the punches, and I had to learn that long ago. I can be really hard on myself, so for a long time I believed that even if no one else could get the balance right, surely *I* could. It took me hundreds of conversations with women in my chair, plus the wisdom that comes with hard-earned life experience, to finally realize that not only does true balance not exist, but it only gets harder. The older you get, the more jobs you take on, without (usually) giving up anything. Getting married? Another job. Maintaining a social life is a job. Having kids is a HUGE job. Taking care of your own health and well-being is a job. And later you might add caring for aging parents to that list. And of course there's the actual job that pays actual money.

I don't think I truly accepted that I couldn't do it all, and that I didn't even want to, until I had that panic attack. Until then, I'd always had this nagging feeling of urgency that I wasn't doing everything I needed to—that I was forgetting something—but that day flipped a switch in me. I finally accepted that there was no such thing as doing it all, and that it was time to put even more trust in my people and my teams. And here's the other thing about "doing it all." Even if it *were* possible, it's not worth it. Being an overachiever and a busybody is as much a curse as it is a blessing. I've looked back over my work schedule of the past twenty years a lot while writing this book, and what I see doesn't always make me feel proud—sometimes it just makes me feel like a lunatic. No part of me is thinking, *Good for you, Jen, for missing your bestie's daughter's first birthday party so you could squeeze in one more client.*

I've long given up the hope of balancing work with personal life, or friends with family. The balance I hope for above all else is to somehow fit in having a life, taking care of myself, and acting with a purpose every single day. But even the word "balance" comes with so much pressure. I truly believe that what's more important than being balanced is being kind to yourself. Practice self-compassion. When you realize you've been working so hard that you've missed another family gathering, forgive yourself. When you've gone on an extended getaway and suddenly feel panicked because you haven't returned a single email, remind yourself that it's okay. You are only one person, and you will fuck up and you will have missteps and you will feel stressed and feel guilty, and you'll have to pick up and keep moving forward. The people who love you will be there when you do. I recently asked Lindsay how she felt about our relationship back when I was in the thick of it—busy and unavailable and probably not being the best friend. I'd never asked her before, probably because I was too scared to hear the answer, but here's what she said: "After the slow realization that I was no longer number one, and after getting over the frustration that at times I couldn't count on you to show up on time or even at all, I came to a place where I could either keep getting annoyed, stop being friends with you, or lower my expectations and just accept the changing friendship for what it was. I chose the latter and eventually came to understand why you were so swamped and knew that it had nothing to do with me or our friendship. You were building an empire and that was all just growing pains. Today I'm just so happy for you and proud of you and all you've accomplished. And I have mad respect for the way you've helped so many along the way and used your platform to break the mold." Swoon.

Life is short. Do the best you can, but don't beat yourself up when you can't.

Dixie High School—Lindsay Johnson and I with our weird highlights—1997

Lindsay and me using our rent money on a
Contempo shopping spree—1998

CHAPTER NINE
I LOVE YOU,
SUZE ORMAN

This is a book about being your best self and finding your purpose, and you will never hear me say that you need a lot of money to do those things. But I'd be fooling myself, and lying to you, if I pretended that for many people "success" wasn't tied to financial security. And while having money is great, more important than *having* it, I think, is having a *healthy relationship* with it. I know this because my finances have changed dramatically over the last twenty years. I've gone from the girl with no cash who couch-surfed through L.A. to the up-and-coming stylist who threw money at bottle service just because she could, to the aspiring business owner who wanted the power to invest in herself, to the grown-ass adult who knows what she doesn't know and hires outside help to make sure she's saving for the future.

When I first moved to L.A., I had no credit card and barely anything in my checking account. Once I started earning a living, I ran to the nearest Chase bank every payday because I was living in overdraft fee hell and subsisting on instant ramen noodles. Today I have a company that is valued in the hundred millions. That's a pretty major change, and over time I had to shift my understanding of money, and my behavior around it, so that I could become financially responsible, both in the office and out. It's important to learn the finer points of finances so that you can talk the talk in business, but in your personal life, too, you really need to walk the walk.

IT STARTS EARLY

I don't need my psychology-for-hairstylists degree to know that my relationship with money—which has had its ups and downs over the years but is now in a good place—was formed in childhood. It was most significantly influenced, for better or worse, by my father. Whenever money was involved, my dad was always teaching us a lesson. Here's a great example: Every Christmas, my mom would get my sisters and me little things for our stockings. My dad would get us . . . an envelope with cash. "Why would I pay full price for presents when everything will be on sale after Christmas?" he'd ask. Then we'd make the hour-and-forty-five-minute drive to Las Vegas to shop the post-holiday sales.

I always had jobs, because my dad made us contribute financially to any major purchase for ourselves. I swept floors at Sizzler and Little Caesars, and folded jeans at DownEast Outfitters in a suburban strip mall. He would explain to me exactly how long I'd need to work in order to afford something (with tax). When I wanted a bike, and later a car, my dad made me sign a contract with a payment plan. He was the bank, and I would make deposits to save up for the purchase, and if I saved a certain amount by a certain date, he would match it. When I got the car, he agreed to cover half as long as I paid for the other half, plus half of the insurance, and there was a contract for that, too.

I found all of this really annoying, and it probably contributed to some irresponsible spending in my early twenties—years that were basically marked by one act of defiance after another. *But* I can also thank my dad for my entrepreneurial spirit. He taught me about turning passions into a business. He's a really talented musician, and for a while he owned a music store. He also loves to travel, and for a while he had a travel agency. Atkin Music and Atkin Travel were both successful businesses in St. George. It's a wonder OUAI isn't named Atkin Hair.

Though I grew up in a solidly middle-class family, I developed an eye for nice things from the start. When I was eight, my parents got me a piggy bank–type box with three slots: spending, saving, and tithing. I was supposed to give the tithing money to the church every Sunday, but the truth is I turned in empty envelopes and used my tithing money for Hello Kitty eraser boxes and jelly sandals at the mall. I didn't know that my parents would have a meeting with our bishop at the end of the year to learn how much each person in the family had given, and when they found out I was stealing from the Lord to buy shoes . . . well, they were none too pleased.

My eye for nice things extended, unfortunately but unsurprisingly, to coveting other people's good fortune. Every Christmas in Utah, my family would drive through the fancy neighborhood nearby to look at the houses with the amazing light displays. I know it was supposed to be a festive tradition, but whenever we got back to my house after admiring the others, I felt a real letdown. I imagined the lives of the kids in those houses, and the fancy presents waiting for them under their blinged-out trees. Those kids weren't opening envelopes of cash on Christmas morning, they were getting all the coolest, most expensive toys and clothes. Those families had what I thought we lacked or what I thought I wanted. (I know now that this is what society does to everyone. I had a perfectly nice, warm home and grew up in a world of white privilege, but of course we learn at a young age to start coveting what other people have.)

My outlook shifted a little when we moved to Hawaii. We lived among families who were mostly poor in terms of wealth or material things, but they were truly happy people. Living there, it finally got through to me that happiness isn't about having stuff but about having family, tradition, and love. (To be clear, my parents always told me as much, but when you're determined to buy Hello Kitty, you don't always listen to Mom and Dad.) Still, I was a kid who wanted nice things who grew into a teenager and twenty-something who wanted nice things. And the one lesson my father forgot to teach me, because he didn't think it would ever be relevant, was an important one: how to use credit cards.

My father was so financially responsible that he didn't even *have* credit cards when I was growing up. He bought his houses and cars with cash. I think he honestly thought that I would never get a card, so he never taught me anything about interest rates or what "buy now, pay later" really meant. They didn't teach that in high school, either, though it would have been a lot more useful than some of the domestic trades I was learning in Home Economics.* All of this is to say, the minute I moved out of the house I was like, OMG! Credit cards! I thought qualifying for a credit card also qualified me to have new clothes and bags. All. The. Time.

Sadly, that was not the case.

YOUNG, DUMB, AND BROKE

When Lindsay and I arrived in L.A., we knew nothing. Nothing about the city, nothing about money, nothing about how to make it on our own. I don't entirely regret that, because it made those early years formative and memorable ones, but certainly I could have landed on my feet much sooner if I'd had a better handle on what I was getting into. Remember, in the year 2000, people didn't use websites to find apartments the way they do now. We used Thomas Guides—literal paperback books of maps—to find our way around. It's a good thing we could barely read a map, because a few times we tried to go window-shopping on Rodeo Drive in Beverly Hills and ended up instead on Rodeo Road, pronounced like the sport, in Culver City. We couldn't really afford decent housing, so we looked in the classifieds for shared rentals and came pretty close to living on a boat in Long Beach with a random guy and his

---

* *Turns out, I don't need to know the difference between a running stitch and a cross-stitch.*

dog. Luckily we found a different roommate with a one-bedroom apartment, and the three of us shared the rent, Lindsay and I sleeping in beds that we lofted on cinder-blocks in order to create storage space underneath. We bought a black pleather couch from Salvation Army that was ripped all over, and we colored in bald spots with Sharp-ies. Tito's Tacos, not far from our place, basically kept us nourished—except for our monthly fancy dinners at California Pizza Kitchen, a splurge that required weeks of saving up. Our other treat was going to Forever 21 and trying on clothes. We couldn't afford to buy anything, but just being in there felt like stepping through the gates of crop-top heaven.

When we started working odd jobs and *really* wanted to treat ourselves, Lindsay and I would save up for months to buy concert tickets. We both loved music (this was my Dave Matthews partner-in-crime, after all), so we would buy nosebleed seats at a big arena and, right before the concert started, we'd finagle our way to the front, taking whatever empty seats we could find. We'd keep moving a few rows up and a few more rows up until we ultimately found a way to sneak backstage (this was before they had ticket scanners, and backstage lists were on paper). Long before I was doing hair behind the scenes at live shows, I was sneaking my way backstage at Beck and Coldplay and Smashing Pumpkins concerts.

It was during those early days in that one-bedroom apartment that I got my first credit card. I feel stupid when I think about it now, but when you are a nineteen-year-old who wants to feel like an adult and there's a credit card in your mailbox and all you have to do is call a number to activate it, it's like free money. (What you probably already know, and I learned eventually: there is no such thing as free money. Thank you for coming to my TED Talk.) I honestly thought those cards would be my way out—I'd get a credit card, spend now, pay later. NBD.

For a while, I lived on my new cards. A trip to the Bahamas? Lindsay and I charged it. We bought new clothes and stocked our wine closet. Plus, it was good to build credit, right? That's what all the financial experts said. Having the credit cards made us feel like we could survive, like we had a safety net, but by the time I was twenty-two, I was about $17,000 in debt. I had fifteen different credit cards, and I would charge $2,000 here, another $2,000 there. I should have known better—I mean, my father spent my entire childhood teaching me how to set up payment plans and only buy what I could afford—but it was all too tempting. Eventually I got a job and started working on paying off the debt, but as anyone who has been in significant credit card debt can attest, it's like drowning in quicksand—every time you think you're getting closer to safety, you start sliding backward. Debt like that can have serious negative effects on your ability to get a home or a job or even a cell phone contract. I was working paycheck to paycheck, barely able to pay the minimum on my cards, and sending our landlord the rent with notes that said, "Please cash this before we spend it." Ah, youth.

Given the credit card fiasco, you'd think I would have learned the difference between "good" and "bad" spending, but once I started climbing the styling ranks and paying down my debt and actually having some disposable income, my first move was not what it should have been.

What I *should* have done was start saving for a rainy day. But what I did instead was go out partying, springing for VIP tables and bottle service at the hottest clubs. I've got some blurry Polaroids to prove it. I was interacting with celebrities and their assistants at the salon during the day, and when I saw them out at night, I wanted to feel accepted and included. I wasn't buying art or driving a fancy car or living in a nice apartment. But when it came to socializing, I was making stupid decisions. To be fair, I was totally unprepared for the nightlife culture. Most people sow their wild oats in high school, but not me. I'd never smoked weed, touched coffee, or had a sip of alcohol, so it took some time to get all those new experiences under my belt and out of my system. (Though I still don't know why I thought it was so cool to purchase an entire bottle of alcohol at a club instead of just ordering a drink.) The point is: once I had a little bit of money, I really sucked at saving it.

The only smart thing I did with my money in those days was to invest in my kit—wigs and hair extensions and all the best tools, because I knew that if I was prepared for any look, I could do any job I was asked to do, and that kind of preparedness would pay off in the long run. I'm proud that even while I made some immature choices about my free time and extra money, I somehow knew that investing in my career would eventually pay off.

FINANCE 101: PAY ATTENTION

When I was twenty-three, I received the best business lesson I ever could have asked for: I was promoted to manager at Estilo. I still can't believe I got promoted as quickly as I did, but I wasn't going to forgo my chance to move up and learn and do more. I wanted to prove to myself that I was capable of tackling things I wasn't comfortable with, and I wanted to show the salon owners who instilled their faith in me that I wouldn't let them down.

I soaked up so much knowledge during that stint. Not only did I get to witness the creative process that goes into sending a client out the door with a smile and newfound confidence, but I learned about the financials of the hairstyling industry, and I got to see what the margins were on the products we sold, and how much money different services brought in, and what every stylist made for the year. I learned about bookkeeping and what it takes to run a salon. I learned that hairstylists can be prickly, because creatives like to be recognized for their talent, and that sometimes they're so focused on that acknowledgment that they forget about the more practical parts of the job, like paying taxes or making sure their licenses are up-to-date. Those lessons came in real handy later on, when I wanted to work for myself and hire other professionals. This kind of knowledge is there for the taking no matter what your industry, as long as you're paying attention. Let's say you're just starting out as a young real estate agent—you can learn sales tactics from other agents, sure, but you can also learn about industry trends from landlords, or about new, up-and-coming businesses from tenants, which will in turn lead to landing bigger deals and getting bigger commissions. The numbers side of things can feel intimidating, but the more you watch and learn, the easier it becomes.

I truly saw, during those Estilo days, that if you aren't

responsible with your money, it can disappear faster than you made it. So many of our insanely talented stylists struggled when it came to managing their personal finances. They figured that their success would never fade, so they bought expensive clothes and spent on partying and traveling, and then suddenly a slow season would hit and eat up their modest savings. Watching all this play out, I knew I wanted to avoid making any more mistakes than I already had. I guess you could say it scared me straight—I quit ordering $100 bottles of vodka and started to pay off my debt and build a nest egg.* Even today, no matter my company's valuation, I know the cash could go away tomorrow, and that fact is a major motivator. I'm not sitting pretty with my feet up on the desk; I'm working hard so that the company and the people who rely on me will continue to thrive and feel proud of what we've built.

SPEND MONEY TO SAVE MONEY: HIRING FINANCIAL HELP

As my career progressed and I realized what it took to succeed and how much I wanted to invest in myself— paying my own way to fly to Paris for Fashion Week, or

* *Before COVID-19 hit the U.S., I'd always seen hairstyling as a job that had security. No one imagined that there would come a time when we weren't allowed to have the salons open or do house calls. It was a major wake-up call to the hairstylist community about how important it is to have savings.*

splurging on the best styling tools—I got smarter about my money. Paying full price for a sweater or dropping hundreds of dollars at a club seemed ridiculous when I was trying to save for my next round-trip ticket. Clearly, I was becoming more like my father, and as it turned out, that was a pretty great thing.

Unfortunately, this new attitude about money was not enough to save me from being audited in 2007, the first year I started styling on my own. Hairdressers get targeted for audits a lot since our income fluctuates so much, but that year the IRS came after me for $125,000. When I saw that number I panicked, but luckily a few other glam squad friends who'd been through similar experiences showed me the ropes. They recommended a money manager, Melissa Morton, who had helped them through similar situations. Melissa was a lifesaver. Not only did she help me survive the audit, but, even better, she showed me how to get my finances under control. She educated me on everything I was doing wrong (there was a lot!) and gave me tips on how to make it right. She showed me the basics: *Here's your allowance per month. Here's what you need to save. Here's what you can spend.* There I was, in my late twenties, paying a business manager to remind me of all the things my dad used to school me on for free.

Getting audited for a crazy amount of money was a major "oh, shit" moment for me—it was a loud and clear message that I had to get my act together. I can say now that I'm glad it happened, though, because hiring Melissa as my business manager was one of the smartest decisions I've ever made. I needed someone to teach me everything I'd never

learned, like writing off expenses, and setting up a corpo-
ration, and what to pay for in cash, and the best approach
to taxes, and how to establish an allowance. Melissa is the
one who explained to me that, while I might want a Gucci
bag, I have to keep in mind that the bag basically costs
twice the purchase price, because I'll need to work double
the hours to get that money back. She taught me that small
changes—investing in an espresso machine and skipping
Starbucks, that sort of thing—save big money. Eventually
she took charge of my bookkeeping and accounting and
my long- and short-term investments. And she has advised
me on everything from preparing budgets to selling and
acquiring real estate. She helped Mike and me streamline
our accounts to one credit card with a spending limit. If we
want to make a major purchase, we consult with her first.
Plus, we meet quarterly to review our finances and discuss
what we could do better.

I'm telling you all this not to promote Melissa's services,
but because I can't stress enough how valuable it is to have
some level of financial guidance from someone who really knows what she's doing. Not everyone needs a full-on
business manager right out of the gate, but I know how
tempting it is to dismiss the idea of paying someone to
take care of your money. It's easy to think that you'd rather
keep your earnings and handle the cash yourself. It's a
reasonable idea . . . except that in the long run, an actual
expert will save you so much more than the 5 percent or
3 percent or whatever it is the person charges you. And
as your career continues to evolve, this kind of guidance
becomes increasingly valuable. You always think that the
next big step is the one that's going to make you happy,

but it also always comes with more responsibility. When I was eighteen, I couldn't believe that I could even get a credit card. But now I have a whole team of employees with credit cards that are tied to *my* bank account, and we pay attention to our finances in a way that I avoided when I was young.

Aside from serving as a tour guide through the money maze, outside financial advisers *really* come in handy if you're considering mixing business with pleasure . . . and by that I mean doing any sort of financial deal with friends or family, or even just doing work *for* those people. Money managers can help you make decisions early on in your partnership that can protect you should things go south. Or you can outsource to them any difficult conversations that you'd rather not have. I do a lot of styling work for women I consider friends, and sometimes it feels uncomfortable to ask your pal to pay up. I'm lucky to have representation that handles a lot of the financial logistics with my clients and the brands I work with, so that I'm saved from having to knock on doors asking for money I'm owed. If you find yourself in a position where the line between business and pleasure is getting fuzzy, it's worth considering hiring someone to outsource the money stuff.

Remember: you can't be good at everything—building your business *and* managing your relationships *and* growing your social following *and* managing your money—so if you have the opportunity to get some help with financial planning from an expert, by all means PLEASE do it. Just know that when you do, they probably won't support your Uber and Postmates habits. I still get yelled at about those.

THINGS I LEARNED THE HARD WAY

want this book to help you skip the line and teach you the things it took me decades to learn, and so I asked Melissa what she thought were the most important things for anyone to understand about money management. Obviously the advice she offers below isn't specific to your financial situation, and it can't take the place of a personal financial adviser, but I hope it will offer you an introductory education that I never had. Hey, maybe it will even help you avoid the audit and the credit card debt and the 1942 tequila bottle charges.

Melissa's Money Management 101

- Invest in your values and your future—yourself, your family, your business, your home, your education—not in things.
- Student loan debt is not bad debt. Do what it takes to make your payments, but don't stress about paying it off earlier than you need to.
- Once you've paid off a debt or a major investment (house, car), celebrate your hard work and responsible planning! Then slide that part of your budget into another smart spot, like a mortgage payment or a savings account. If you didn't miss that money before, you won't miss it now.
- ALWAYS pay your taxes. ALWAYS. Don't ignore any notices. Don't file for an extension. Move through the anxiety and get help if you need it. Paying fees to a good money manager or tax accountant will save you money in the long term.

- Start small. Save what you can, even if it's ten dollars a week. As you start to make more money or get a raise or a promotion, increase that amount. Just try it. You'll be surprised at how quickly it adds up.
- People save more when they don't have to think about it. Set up an automatic monthly payment into your savings account or get an app that rounds up purchases and moves the change into your savings. Set it, forget it, and then take a look at your balance at the end of the year. You will be amazed.
- Get good insurance—homeowners, renters, health, auto, life, all of it. It's a boring subject, but insurance is literally a lifesaver. You can't plan for everything, and a single event out of your control can be completely devastating.
- Pay your credit card balances in full every month. If you can't, use a debit card that's attached to its own checking account. Set up a weekly automatic transfer that's within your means, and when the card declines, you're done for the week. Eventually you'll develop an intuition about how much you can spend, but don't take off the training wheels before you're ready.
- The only person who can change your habits is you. Even the best business managers in the world can't stop you from swiping away your funds. Have the courage to look at your accounts regularly and take accountability for your choices.

THAT EFF-YOU MONEY

During my days of managing Estilo, I wasn't just learning about how money flows in and out of a salon, I was also observing how money affects people. I had plenty of wealthy clients who were very obviously unhappy, and I also had plenty of colleagues who let their success get the best of them and ended up becoming entirely different people. They got so powerful in their own heads that it became impossible for them to check their egos at the door. Blinded by a little bit of material success, they suddenly (and probably unintentionally) stopped listening to anyone else in their lives and very often drove away the people closest to them. I made a resolution early on that no matter what happened, even if I got super-successful, I would not become that person. I would surround myself with the people who have known me since the beginning, the people who keep me true to myself, and always remain open to their feedback. I didn't want to be someone who lets money or success change who they are.

It was in those moments of watching some of the uber-successful stylists in the salon that I realized I absolutely had to have a passion for my work. *I need to love what I'm doing here*, I thought, *because the minute it stops being fulfilling is the minute I'll get resentful, even if the money is piling up.* I wanted to be sure my self-worth wasn't based on how much money I was making or what designer labels I could afford, and I didn't want the relentlessness of the work to kill my spirit. Listen, I'm not saying you have to love your job all the time—I had years of gigs I wasn't passionate about that helped pay my bills while I was figuring out what my career should be—but if the only benefit is financial, things aren't going to end well. Money isn't worth much if earning it makes you miserable.

I know this all sounds easy for me to say, but it took a lot of hard work and careful planning to get to this place. Now I know that a big part of what financial success means to me is having the ability to invest in my own ideas and my own business—and for a girl who treasures her freedom, that's pretty much the best feeling in the world. I kept Mane Addicts afloat on my own for its first five years of existence, which means the money I was making from doing hair went right back into paying for our team, our office, and travel. I knew it was a risk, but I really believed that the platform would thrive and could become bigger than anyone imagined at the time. And guess what? I was right.

Truth be told, I wish I'd been able to put more of my own capital into OUAI, but the stakes were different. I'm incredibly grateful for the investors we have, but it's always been unnatural to me to ask people for their money, to hope they'll take a risk on me and my idea. And of course, the more investors you have in any business, the more the profit is shared. Most investors are looking to get in on the ground level of a major success story, which means coming in low with the hopes of a big payday down the line. That's why when you're building your own business, there is so much freedom—and financial upside—in being your own investor.

The point is: save your money. Who knows what your next big idea might be, and I want you to have that eff-you money so you don't have to rely on someone else to support your vision. It's hard to fully communicate how powerful that feels, except to say that even when you are a CEO, you answer to your investors. But if you are your own biggest investor . . . well, then, you answer to yourself. The more you invest in yourself, the more you own of your own business. Once you're in the driver's seat, the question becomes less about means and more about how much you believe in yourself.

TREAT YOURSELF (WITHIN REASON, PLEASE)

don't want to be the Scrooge who says you should never celebrate or splurge or buy a latte, and I'm not pretending that I'm immune to enjoying the finer things in life. When my finances changed enough that I could start to afford some of the luxury items my clients had, I got the designer bug (I'll never forget buying my first Balenciaga bag!) and started investing in an upgraded wardrobe. It's totally okay to reward yourself for your hard work, but I would challenge you to think hard about which rewards might bring a fleeting rush of adrenaline and which ones will bring you real joy. In a corner of my closet, for example, you will find a bunch of designer items that I bought back in the day because I thought they conveyed status or success and they made me feel important. But these items stopped giving me any satisfaction after about two wears, and now I worry they scream *I'm trying to prove something!* These clothes and shoes and bags do not make me feel loved or feel safe. Also you'll soon find most of them on The RealReal, because upcycling actually does bring me a lot of satisfaction.

Other than a few Lorraine Schwartz and Cartier bracelets, most of my "treat yourself" spending is relegated to experiences with family and friends, like concerts or weekend trips (highly recommend!) or services that will pay off in the long term. I absolutely think that investing in your health, whether it's a gym or ClassPass or exercise equipment, is a gift that keeps on giving. Also while retail therapy offers diminishing returns, actual therapy is a much more worthwhile and effective (and *maaayyyybe* even cheaper) investment. I treat myself to massages, too, which is a real kindness to my aching body after I've been on my feet all day, every day. I love going on adventures, and am willing to spend on travel. Those experiences shape who I am as a person, and I hope they'll influence my children one day the way they've influenced me.

This year, I've also come around to the idea of investing in my home. I don't mean the actual real estate (though we've tried to be smart in that regard). I'm talking about the furniture and the vibe and the homeyness of it all. Mike and I moved into our current house in 2019, and it's the first time in my life that we've purchased nice furniture and really focused on creating a pretty and peaceful environment. I've always been super-cheap about home décor, and Goodwill has usually been my interior designer (hello, I lived with two roommates in a one-bedroom apartment for years), but this time we decided to create a space we love and would maybe start a family in. There's a lot to be said for working hard and walking into an actual home at the end of the day that makes you feel safe and happy. Investing time and energy and money in our living space has had such a positive effect on my well-being.

OUR KIDS WILL GROW up with so much more than I ever did, but I can't wait to use the same system of contracts and allowances that my dad did with me. A friend recently told me that every January her dad gave her a year's worth of allowance and said, "Make it last." That's a pretty major responsibility for a kid, but a great way to teach budgeting! I'm into all of it. And while my kids will not be tithing in the biblical sense, they will be obligated to invest some of their money in the world around them— that's non-negotiable, and they will soon learn that giving back to their community feels a whole lot better than owning a giant purse-full of Hello Kitty erasers.

Today, I live about five minutes from the same Chase bank that I used to visit every other Friday, checking my balance and holding my breath in hopes that my next rent check would clear. Our first OUAI billboard went up just a couple blocks from it, too. I like to think that's the universe making sure I appreciate how far I've come. Whenever I drive past that bank, I have a good laugh thinking of my younger self . . . she had so much to learn! But I also get a rush of pride, because today I've created financial security for myself and my family. Knowing that I can provide for people I care about is incredibly comforting. Take it from me: there is no power like that of a financially independent woman.

During a Malibu weekend, taking time off with my loves
Mike, Roo, and Chewy—2020

Giving a presentation for a Dyson hair
tool launch in New York City—2018

CHAPTER TEN
MOVIN' ON UP

At this point in the book, you're privy to most of my secrets when it comes to being your best self or creating your best life. But as you prepare to conquer the world—even if you take everything you've read here and act on all of it—there's still so much that's out of your control. You can't dictate the behavior of others or anticipate world events. The only thing any of us *can* control is how we react to whatever is thrown at us. When stress levels are high, it's natural to become impatient or to react with frustration or anger. But who does that help? Not only do those kinds of responses reflect poorly on you, but living in a state of emotional reactivity is also draining. Trust me, I've lived it and it's not sustainable.

I manage several teams across a few different organizations, so there are inevitably times when plans go awry, or a product doesn't do as well as I'd hoped, or deadlines aren't met—and I judge my performance as a leader by how I react in those moments. It's my responsibility to keep the peace and create an atmosphere of collaboration instead of competition. Rather than responding right away—whether you're an assistant or the CEO—try putting your reaction on ice and waiting until your feelings aren't so heated and you can make a calm decision. Go for a walk, take some deep breaths. No good decisions are made out of fear or anger, and once you unleash on someone there's no taking it back.

I try my best to take the same approach to issues that come up in my marriage or in other close relationships. I'm not always successful—my sense of humor can be dark or cynical, and sometimes I make jokes at the expense of the people closest to me. I want to say I do it all out of love, but I know I use humor as a defense mechanism, to divert attention away from myself. I'm trying to change that behavior. I don't want to be the person sitting around making fun of people, whether it's behind their back or to their face.

When it comes to issues that crop up in the workplace, one thing I've learned is that while it's great to have the support and empathy of the people in the trenches with you, when things go wrong, sharing frustrations can go south quickly. In office environments especially, complaining is like breathing. Bitching about a boss or a colleague with a work friend can feel like a bonding activity, but in reality it usually only makes things worse. Everyone needs to vent and let off steam sometimes, but too much venting with too many people just makes you more fixated on the problem.

Being an empowered woman who knows her worth means filling your orbit with relationships that give you energy—you want to feel revitalized, not drained, after spending time with the people you care about. (Especially if you're short on "friend time," which, let's be real, aren't we all?) It also means you might have to let go of friendships, professional and personal, that wear you down rather than lift you up, because ultimately your focus should be on cultivating relationships that support your goals rather than distract from them.

There are about a zillion different reasons you might choose to cool off a friendship. Maybe the person is super-negative and complains about everything all the time, or they constantly find themselves in dysfunctional romantic relationships that they love to talk about but never want to change. I get frustrated when people complain about problems when the obvious solution is right in front of their faces, but everyone gets where they need to be in their own time. I've learned that you can't take on other people's baggage or fix their problems for them. I truly believe you are the sum of the people you hang out with, and you have to have the instinct for self-preservation if you want to stay healthy, let alone be successful.

So what do you do when you have someone in your life, work or personal, who's constantly fueling the fires of negativity and draining your energy? Ending a relationship of any kind, even if it's toxic, is really hard. It usually involves an awkward conversation in which you have to say something along the lines of, "I can't be who you want me to be right now." I'm not gonna lie, that conversation isn't fun. But it's necessary, because while being a great friend is a wonderful quality, at the end of the day *you have to have your own back*. You have to create boundaries. It's been my experience that the upside of those hard conversations is not only a saner life but also real personal growth. You'll hear yourself say, "No, this relationship isn't working for me," and then you'll look in the mirror and be like, *Whoa, who is that grown-up?* That's a moment to be proud of.

BUT FIRST, FORGIVE

I've been around a lot of drama in my life—being in the salon around so many people and working with high-profile clients, it comes with the territory. One thing I've noticed just from bearing witness to it is that the kind of behavior we dismissively refer to as "drama" is often the reaction of people who've been deeply hurt at some point in their lives and who haven't been able to let go of that pain. Resentment and bitterness are toxic, and left unresolved they will affect your behavior and your relationships across the board.

I can't speak for everybody's pain or life circumstances, but for me, learning to forgive has been incredibly healing and transformative. At this point in my life, I've lived away from my parents for as long as I lived with them, but until recently I still blamed them for a lot. So many religious lessons that I didn't agree with were drilled into my head as a kid, and I definitely had some residual resentment about the influence those lessons had on my life. (If you've heard the song "Spooky Mormon Hell Dream" from *The Book of Mormon*, you know what I mean.) What I've come to understand is that my parents are just two human beings who got married really young and were doing the best they could, and what they truly thought was right. And they were—and are!—incredible parents, even if we don't always see eye to eye. Once I accepted that, I was able to let go of the pain and love my family for who they are. Mike and I recently went to Utah for a visit, and it was so invigorating to be back where I grew up and to ask my parents questions about my family. I don't want to be one of those people who walks through life angry about the past or cynical about her childhood, so it was really nice to spend time in St. George, looking at old photos and enjoying the beautiful scenery without contaminating the experience with bitterness about stuff that went down when I was an angry fifteen-year-old.

Forgiving family members is really hard, because most of us see our relatives—those people who push all our most sensitive buttons—year after year. Even if we *were* trying to forgive and forget, it would be impossible, because there's that reminder, every . . . single . . . holiday. Old wounds get reopened, and healing takes longer. It's a lot easier to let go of a grudge against, say, an old coworker, someone you may never see again after leaving the job. But one of the most powerful moments of forgiveness in my life actually stemmed from a dispute with a business partner, and it felt just as emotional and high-stakes as any resolution I've had with my family.

It happened, as so many of these fallouts do, after I went into business with a friend. Things were fine for a bit, but suddenly we found ourselves at a crossroads—a lot of money was at stake, and we couldn't seem to agree on anything. I felt hurt and betrayed and angry. My business partner probably felt the same way, though I can't speak for them. It got messy, lawyers got involved, and we didn't really speak for a year and a half. It was ugly. But the worst part had nothing to do with the money. The worst part was that I lost a friend. It took me a long time, and a decent amount of therapy, to realize that holding on to the anger was hurting me more than it was hurting my partner. Ever heard the saying "I'm drinking poison so YOU die"? I didn't like the bitterness I was holding on to, and I knew the only way to change the situation was to approach my former friend from a place of love and ask to be forgiven, and offer forgiveness in return.

And so, not too long ago, I apologized—both for my actions and my reactions. They weren't calm, and I certainly shouldered some blame for the way our relationship spiraled. I reacted to the situation the same way I reacted in high school when my dad tried to discipline me. I claimed it wasn't fair. I behaved like a child. And I'm not saying I didn't have a right to be upset, but it was time to move on from anger. It was hard—forgiving someone takes courage and strength—but I decided to engage empathy and love rather than anger and resentment, and that allowed me to see the bigger picture. Guys, this is why therapy is so important.

The moment I apologized, the heavy lump in the pit of my stomach disappeared. We hugged and cried, and it felt great. It's one of the moments in my life that I'm most proud of, because I took action and changed the course of that relationship. Apologizing or forgiving can feel intimidating, but tackling the scary things head-on gives us strength. My relationship with my former business partner may never go back to the way it was, but that's okay. I think we'll both be happy not to lug around the baggage anymore.

Forgiveness is a powerful thing—not only can I attest to the fact that it makes you feel like a weight has been lifted, but studies have linked forgiveness to reduced anxiety and depression, lowered stress levels, and even lower mortality rates. I think some of that potent healing power comes from the fact that it's not easy—forgiveness takes a lot of work and self-reflection. Our natural instinct tends to be to deflect our feelings onto someone else or try to change someone rather than forgive them. Forgiveness means accepting our own faults and accepting other people as they are, or accepting their actions as they were, no "fixing" required. Who hasn't tried to change someone they're dating so that they could fit the mold of "the one"? It's bad for everyone involved—the "fixer" ends up disappointed, and the person who supposedly needs to be fixed feels, well, pretty shitty. No one wants to be on the other side of the unsolicited makeover. It never feels great to be told you're not enough.

It's very common for clients in my chair to tell me all the reasons they're annoyed at their partner that day. I let them go on and get it out and do their venting, but at the end of the conversation I like to ask one question. *What do you like about him/her?* Everyone is always taken aback, but then they start listing the good stuff, and their face changes and their mood lifts and they light up. For whatever reason, it's easier to point out a partner's flaws than it is to flag their good traits, but taking the time to reflect on why you like someone is a helpful reminder not to take them for granted. Plus, if you tell someone what you love about them or what they do that makes you laugh or smile, they're going to want to do those things more often, because everyone likes to be praised. Focusing on the positive begets more positive. Try being the light instead of pushing someone to see the light.

USE THAT MUTE BUTTON

The Mute button is the single best thing that has ever been created in the world of social media. It's like being able to leave a party without having to say goodbye.* When you mute, you spare the hurt feelings of an "unfollow," but still see only what you *want* to see. You can mute all the hustle porn or the false modesty or the negativity and have a feed full of puppy content. We can't control all the drama that comes into our lives, but if there's a person in your feed who constantly rubs you the wrong way or whom you're constantly judging, you DO control whether or not you witness their constant updates. I know it can be enticing to cling to those accounts—there's a sort of rush that comes with getting all hyped up and feeling collectively horrified at someone's online behavior—but living a life of positivity feels a lot better. If you find pleasure in making fun of people's workout posts or long stories or OOTD pics, you've probably got some self-love work to do.

Whenever possible, I might suggest taking it one step further than the Mute button. Marie Kondo your feed and unfollow the people that don't spark joy. Let your social media be something that delights you. Following 2,000 people is completely overwhelming—you could spend your entire day trying to get through it all. I used to hide under a blanket and look at Instagram for hours during the movies.† Now I know better. Aside from being a total waste of time, that kind of behavior kept me from actually experiencing my own life. I mean, I was *at the movies.* I'd literally paid money to sit in front of a screen, and yet I couldn't

---

* *Which I know may sound rude, but sometimes it's the only way. Saying goodbye to everyone at a party can take up to a good hour.*
† *I also used to keep my finger on the screen of my phone at all times because I was so anxious about losing my place. I'm legit embarrassed to admit that now, but cheers to honesty.*

pull myself away from the feed. These days I don't let myself follow more than four hundred people, but even that can feel like too much sometimes.

It's important to note that there's a difference between muting or unfollowing someone and canceling them entirely. It's become trendy to "cancel" people when they mess up, but it's unhelpful and unfair to deny people the opportunity to grow from their mistakes. In cancel culture, everyone's so caught up in exposing wrongdoers that they overlook the chance to teach someone how to do better. We all mess up—try to be a part of someone's efforts toward change rather than burying them. Before you write someone off, give them a chance to grow.

YOUR BEST AUTHENTIC SELF

There's so much to keep track of these days. What we should do, what we shouldn't do, what we want to do, what we have to do, who we should follow, who we want to be. If you've read this book, it's probably because you want to find your purpose, pursue your passions, find success doing what you love, and live your life to its fullest expression. But those goals can only be achieved when you follow your gut and remain true to yourself. In the performative, filtered, Facetuned world we live in today, authenticity can be hard to come by, and harder even to understand. What does it even mean to "be yourself" anymore? At its core, I believe authenticity is about self-awareness. Understanding who *you* are, and honoring that truth, rather than just following trends or taking cues from influencers. It's great to take advice and best practices and inspiration from people you admire, but their path is not yours. Figure out what it is that you like to do or wear or listen to, and don't change that to fit anything you've been told is cool or attractive or even sellable. Your life should not be dictated by a viral hashtag or social media campaign or validation from other people.

What's funny is that the further we stray, as a society, from authenticity, the trendier that word becomes, probably because it's so rare. But broadcasting your authenticity is pretty much the opposite of actually being authentic. Instead of posting your #nofilter photo or making a big deal about sharing your #nomakeup selfie, just do you. Rather than trying to cash in on a trend, accept who you are and share that person with the world. Because, I'll tell you, social media has really fine-tuned people's bullshit detectors, so if you're out there faking it, your followers will know.

In business, authenticity has served me well. I've said already that I did things differently from the start—sharing pics, offering tutorials, promoting other people's stuff—because that's just who I was, and I trusted myself. I couldn't deny what I believed, in my gut, was a better way. Being competitive and secretive just isn't me, and pretending otherwise would have felt horrible.

One thing that the disruptors and innovators who've made a mark in business have in common—and I like to believe I belong somewhere in that category—is that we've gone our own way rather than just doing what's always been done. So trust your instincts, believe in your ideas, and be true to who you are. And once that authenticity leads to success, remember what got you there and try to use your influence to help others. You can throw out the entire list of dos and don'ts that I've recommended as long as you follow this one rule: don't forget who you are right now, and no matter what success comes your way, stay connected to that person. Be authentic to yourself.

One of the highest compliments I've ever received came just recently, after my father decided to watch my YouTube channel. He called me up after a few episodes. "Hey BZ," he said. That's what he calls me, because I was a busy bee as a kid. "I found your YouTube channel, and I was waiting for you to turn it on for the camera, and it never happened. I was watching and it was just you, it was my BZ." That kind of acknowledgment, from the man who has known me and loved me since the beginning . . . it was everything.

WHAT'S NEXT IS UP TO YOU

It's my hope that you will walk away from this book with the tools to create your own happiness, but that doesn't mean every day of your life is going to be a great one. It's healthy to feel angry or sad or scared sometimes. We are human beings with human emotions, and resisting or denying those feelings only gives them power. But keep in mind that emotions last about ninety seconds, so don't get too stuck in them. You have to be able to take the bad with the good, and sometimes I worry that social media has tricked us into believing that for "successful" people, things are just always good. I promise you that's not the case. Feel your feelings, and remember that when you emerge on the other side of those darker moments, you'll be stronger and smarter and more equipped to handle the next obstacle. No one wants to live on an emotional roller coaster, but resilience and the ability to weather the tough times are defining characteristics of the happiest people.

I've done my best in these pages to share all the things I wish someone had told me back when I was just starting out but also when I was in the thick of it, busting my ass trying to establish myself in a complicated and exclusive industry. And while my path took me into hairstyling and then into entrepreneurship, the guidebook looks the same no matter your passion. Approach every day with confidence, and push through to earn a seat at the table—you deserve to go after your dreams. Never lose sight of the power of being a good person. Work hard and put in your time—nothing happens overnight. Don't make the work about you, and remember that strong relationships are the key to getting ahead. Set goals and live your values. Resist getting blinded by the dollar, but do know your worth. Be honest about what you want and go after it, even if— *especially* if—what you want changes over the course of your journey. And most of all, be kind to yourself. Don't run yourself into the ground. Take a break every now and then. Connect with other people. Help others rise up with you. Breathe.

Your career and your relationships and your own emotional growth—it's all in your hands. You can read this book from start to finish, memorize it if you want or post your favorite quotes on social (tag me), but only you can turn these lessons into action or tailor them to fit your journey. You are in control, even if sometimes it doesn't feel that way . . . which is pretty effing exciting when you think about it. You decide what happens next.

I'm going to tell you the same thing I tell my assistants when they move on to their next challenge and embark on the next step of their career: go out there and surprise yourself. After twenty years, I continue to be surprised by where life takes me, and if I'd stuck to only what I knew I could do or what I had planned, my life would look a lot different right now. Surprising yourself means you're taking smart risks and not repeating the same mistakes. Hell, I'm surprising myself in this very moment. Because I just wrote a book. A whole entire book. I never thought that I could or would do such a thing, and I still can't believe it happened, but here I am, checking this off my bucket list.

No matter how successful we are, deep down, we all feel like the new kid in town, just trying to figure our shit out. Here's a piece of advice from my mom that's always worked for me: Remember who you are and what you stand for. I hope you will shrug off any doubts and go after the life you dream of, even if everyone around you is telling you to do the opposite. Even if you've never seen anyone do whatever it is you want to do. Take a chance, cut out the doubt, and put in the work. You are worth it. See where you end up in the next five, ten years. It probably won't be where you expected, but I hope it makes you proud.

I'm Jen Atkin, and I approve this message.

Backstage at *Ellen* with Kim Kardashian West —2017

Touching up Gwen Stefani —2012

Doing a look while on vacay with Chrissy Teigen—2019

Taking a break on set with Khloé Kardashian—2015

ACKNOWLEDGMENTS

To the incredible women who have inspired me, helped guide me, and made me a little bit relevant. I have had the pleasure to burn their hair while they taught me so much about love and life during our glam sessions. Watching these powerhouses navigate their own success, relationships, and children so modestly has truly been an honor. Thank you to these friends and perfect specimens:

Kim Kardashian. Thank you for teaching me to stay in my own lane, to not be f'ing rude, and to go after the life I deserve. I owe so many of my blessings to you, you truly changed my life, and thank you for my avatar moment in the *Kim Kardashian: Hollywood* game.

Kris Jenner. The way you and your daughters have blasted through the iron doors and altered the conversation in both the fashion and beauty industries gives so many of us new opportunities and the courage to find our own voices. Throughout all of your skyrocketing success, you've always made kindness a priority and your girls are the same. You have not only changed my life, but you truly are empowering women around the world. I'm *so* grateful to have you as a mentor, and to have your cell.

My clients and friends. Beauty isn't the *only* thing they have to offer. They are independent, strong, fierce, and graceful. They are juggling careers, school, children, and their relationships. They're standing up for what they believe in, starting movements, and paving the way for future generations. Thank you to: Kourtney Kardashian, Kendall Jenner, Kylie Jenner, Katy Perry, Gwen Stefani, Jennifer Lopez, Hailey Bieber, Gigi Hadid, Bella Hadid, Cindy Crawford, Kaia Gerber, Jessica Alba, Reese Witherspoon, Kelly Rowland, Christina Hendricks, Mindy Kaling, Lily Aldridge, Rosie Huntington Whitley, Kat Dennings, Minka Kelly, Kaley Cuoco, Lily Collins, Karlie Kloss, Nicole Richie, Shay Mitchell, Sofia Vergara, Emma Stone, Jenna Dewan, Emily Ratajkowski, Britney Spears, Jessica Stam, Erin Wasson, and Irina Shayk.

My north stars, Chrissy Teigen and Khloé Kardashian. I'm still mad you guys came to that weird dinner honoring me. I love you both so much and have loved watching you go after life and become such incredible mommies. Thank you for your constant support, belly laughs, and tags through the years. I owe you both a career-push present.

Thank you to my angel agents at Blended Strategy Group, Allison Statter, Sherry Jhawar, Mackenzie Harkins, and Jen Kelly, for your constructive criticism, creative advice, and support. You've been a huge part of my career dreams coming true, and I will forever be grateful for you all. Thank you for helping me navigate and define true success. There was nothing more terrifying for me than going from a salon and being a celebrity hairstylist to being a "budding entrepreneur," and you all helped make it happen.

My best friend/sister since middle school, Lindsay Johnson Goldfine. Thank you for being by my side for the last thirty years. You are my rock, my confidante, my sister. I love that I have someone who shares 75 percent of life memories with me. From getting in trouble in pre-algebra to caramel apple martinis at the Abbey to watching your kids be awesome little humans. I wouldn't be where I am today if it wasn't for your true friendship, awkward haircuts, and your unconditional love. I hope we are dancing together until we're ninety. SkittilyBodilyDoooo. Who is this? Chicken Crap.

To my mentors and friends who helped me along the way with many, many phone calls. Lorraine Schwartz, I can't express how much of a light you are to the people in your life. Thank you for truly changing my life. You taught me how 2BHappy while successful. Also, Andrea Lieberman, Sonia Kashuk, Anastasia Soare, Pat McGrath, Bobbi Brown, Charlotte Tilbury, Katherine Powers, Emily Weiss, Luis Balaguer, Virgil Abloh, Michaeline Heydari, Chloe Fogel, Dana Gardner, Huda and Mona Kattan, Sara Riff, Wendy Rosenthal, Stephanie Shepard, Hillary Kerr, Kelly Patricof, Sophia Rossi, Rachel Zoe, Christophe Robin, Raissa Gerona, Shani Darden, Desi Perkins, Aimee Song, Shayla Mitchell, Katy De Groot, Camila Coehlo, Negin Mersalehi, Marianna Hewitt, Rosetta Getty, Amanda Silverman, April McDaniels, Fajer Fahad, Ashleaha Gonzales, Charlotte Ronson, Lexy Roche, and John Galliano.

To the female hair artists before me who have been my heroes all of these years, Odile Gilbert and Sally Hershberger. I owe so much to them for helping open the door for me in what's been a male-dominated industry for so long. Also, Tracy Cunningham, Kim Kimble, and Rita Hazan.

To the male hairstylists who let me into their magical world and gave me the opportunity to learn from them: Reny Salomon, Philip Carreon, Robert Ramos, Chris McMillan, Renato Campora, Guido Palau, Danilo, and my mentor Andy Lecompte.

To my fellow women in hair Lacy Redway, Riawna Capri, Jenny Cho, Laura Polko, Nikki Nelms, Mara Rozak, Jen Yepez, Ursula Stephen, Priscilla Valles, Justine Marjan, Bridget Brager, Kristen Ess, Cassondra Kaeding, Sarah Potempa . . . CHEERS ladies!!! This one is for all of you! I'm so proud of you!

To my glam fam I've grown up with. Mary Phillips you are a class act and a forever friend. Mario Dedivanovic, I'm so proud of you, and I love you. Also, Marni Senofonte, Kayleen McAdams, Rachel Goodwin, Fiona Stiles, Monica Blunder, Vincent Oquendo, Gregory Arlt, Lauren Anderson, Jamie Greenberg, Beau Nelson, Hrush, Ariel Tejada, Molly Stern, Tom Bachik , Kimmy Keys, Karla Welch, Monica Rose, Johnny Wujek, Rob Zangardi, Mariel Hann, Nicolas Bru, Tara Swennen, Maeve Riley, Jill Jacobs, Brad Goreski, Todd Delano, Vanessa Scali, Troy Surrat, Sir John, Etienne Ortega, Andrew Fitzsimmons, Ash Holm, Jesus Guerrero, Cesar Ramirez, Christian Wood, Harry Josh, Anh Co Tran, Vernon Francois, Scotty Cunha, Chad Wood, Jorge Serrano, George Papanikolas, Mimi Cuttrell, and David Von Cannon.

My online community of followers and fans who have been with me while I figured out how to turn my hobby into a career and a business. Your encouraging comments, DMs, messages, and likes motivated me to keep going in times when I felt like it was too much hard work to handle. So much has changed since 2012, and I owe it all to you for your support in all of my endeavors. We've grown up together, and so much of my success is because of you guys.

To future hairstylists out there: I hope to inspire you all to be your best. Now you have a job: Because of your new tech savvy generation, the old guard sitting in boardrooms can't ignore you anymore. The future of this industry is yours. I know your generation will be the one to not just concentrate on the dollar signs, but also to think about helping others as you get success. You will make the world a better, smarter place.

Thank you to Julie Will for giving me the confidence to tell my story and for allowing me to realize I'm forty and not twenty-five years old, so now really is the time. Your patience and guidance through this process was incredible, and I'm in awe of how enjoyable you made my experience. Thank you. Can we do it again?

To the incredible group of humans at HarperCollins that helped me put my scattered thoughts and distant memories into something substantial. Emma Kupor, Yelena Nesbit, Penny Makras, Bonni Leon-Berman, and Caroline Johnson. If this book is a total flop, I would also like to apologize to these people.

Rachel Bertsche, thank you for holding my hand and bringing my words to life. You're an incredible example of doing it all flawlessly. You not only helped write my story but helped me to see my journey in a way I never had before. Thank you for your patience and sweet spirit through my first time in this process. I'm going to miss our chats and hope this is the first of many books together.

To my assistants and teams at Mane Addicts and OUAI (past and present). Thank you for helping me create and bring my dreams to life. Thank you for your sacrifices, your thoughts and ideas, and for racking up the frequent flyer miles with me. You guys inspire me and make work more fun than it probably should be. Nicole Katsuki, you are my eyes, ears, and brain, and your dedication all these years has meant the world to me.

To my sisters, Kimi and Marci. Thank you Kimi for always loving me and making me feel special. Heavenly Father gave me the best mom, but I also got the best big sister who never let me down. Marci, I'm sorry for all of the fashion shows I forced you to be a part of when you were four years old. You also owe me for all of the looks we created. I'm sorry it took me so long to learn to be a good big sister, but what I lacked I'll make up for in trips and prizes.

To Dad for teaching me that I could do anything in life that I wanted, but I needed to go out and earn it. I think you had me signing contracts at the ripe young age of five? From what my therapists have told me, I've basically become you, and I wouldn't want it any other way. I know I can get through anything in life as long as I listen to music and have a good sense of humor. I know it wasn't always easy listening to my questions and debates, but I hope it was worth it.

To my first feminist hero . . . Mom. Thank you for showing me how to find the best me while in service of others. Thank you for showing me countless Disney movies that have contributed to my warped sense of positivity as an adult. I will never know anyone more loving, forgiving, and encouraging than you. No matter what you were going through in life, you made sure we were OK and always had a smile for us. I still stand by my story that my doll wet the bed on that cruise.

Last but not least, my husband, Mike. Thank you for believing in me, for always encouraging me to trust my gut and to not put up with anyone's bullshit. And, most of all,

thank you for shooting so many campaigns and editorials for *free*. Sure, you're an incredible photographer and director, but what makes me love you most is how much love you have to give the people in your life. I am so honored to be your wife and your partner for life. You've been by my side the past twelve years, and I'm so happy I went to that Oscar party to meet Carlos Lopez's cute Jewish guy friend. I'm so proud of the life we've created together (with dogs), and I love you, Boo Boo.

ABOUT THE AUTHOR

JEN ATKIN is a hairstylist, influencer, and entrepreneur. She is building a beauty empire with cult favorite brand OUAI and editorial destination Mane Addicts. She was named "the most influential hairstylist in the world" by the *New York Times*, and has more than four million social media followers. Jen has worked for more than fifteen years in salons, backstage at Paris and New York Fashion Weeks, and on set with some of the world's biggest celebs, including the Kardashian-Jenners, the Hadids, Gwen Stefani, Chrissy Teigen, Katy Perry, and Jennifer Lopez. When she's not juggling A-list clients and her booming companies, Jen is trying to maintain a personal life at home with her husband and dogs, hiking, meditating, and using funny memes to inspire her followers not to lose their shit.

thank you for shooting so many campaigns and editorials for *free*. Sure, you're an incredible photographer and director, but what makes me love you most is how much love you have to give the people in your life. I am so honored to be your wife and your partner for life. You've been by my side the past twelve years, and I'm so happy I went to that Oscar party to meet Carlos Lopez's cute Jewish guy friend. I'm so proud of the life we've created together (with dogs), and I love you, Boo Boo.

ABOUT THE AUTHOR

JEN ATKIN is a hairstylist, influencer, and entrepreneur. She is building a beauty empire with cult favorite brand OUAI and editorial destination Mane Addicts. She was named "the most influential hairstylist in the world" by the *New York Times*, and has more than four million social media followers. Jen has worked for more than fifteen years in salons, backstage at Paris and New York Fashion Weeks, and on set with some of the world's biggest celebs, including the Kardashian-Jenners, the Hadids, Gwen Stefani, Chrissy Teigen, Katy Perry, and Jennifer Lopez. When she's not juggling A-list clients and her booming companies, Jen is trying to maintain a personal life at home with her husband and dogs, hiking, meditating, and using funny memes to inspire her followers not to lose their shit.